ALEX HALEY

The Man Who
Traced America's
ROOTS

A READER'S DIGEST BOOK

All the stories in this collection have previously appeared in Reader's Digest magazine, except "Aboard the *African Star*," which was transcribed from a live event recorded at the Reader's Digest Association, October 10, 1991.

Editor-in-Chief, Reader's Digest: Jacqueline Leo
Project Editor: Donna G. Banks
Art Director: Hannu Laakso
Photo Researchers: Ilene Bellovin, Linda Carter
Production Director: Stephen Best

Library of Congress Cataloging-in-Publication Data

Haley, Alex.
 [Selections. 2007]
 Alex Haley : the man who traced America's roots.
     p. cm.
 ISBN 978-0-7621-0885-5
1. African Americans—History. 2. African Americans—Social conditions.
3. African Americans—Biography. 4. Haley, Alex. Roots. 5. Haley, Alex.
6. Haley, Alex—Travel. 7. Haley, Alex—Family. 8. African American families.
9. African American historians—Biography. I. Title.
 E185.H26 2007
 973'.0496073—dc22

                                                    2007013365

ISBN-13: 978-0-7621-0885-5

COVER PHOTOS: (HALEY) WILL CROCKETT;
(BERRY) BARRY WETCHER/©2006 REVOLUTION STUDIOS; (KING) SCOTT WEINER

Foreword

When *Reader's Digest* published the first excerpts from Alex Haley's *Roots* in our May and June 1974 issues, we said it was an epic work, "destined to become a classic of American literature." That has proved to be an understatement. In just five months after the book hit stores in 1976, more than one million hardcover copies were purchased. Since then, *Roots* has taken its place among the greatest bestsellers of all time as the number of copies sold has grown to over six million worldwide. Its impact on television was also historic: Some 130 million Americans watched at least part of the 12-hour drama, making it the highest-rated miniseries ever.

But the story of *Roots* started long before a page of the book was written or a frame of the TV drama was filmed. One evening at a lawn party in 1966, Haley met Lila Acheson Wallace, cofounder of *The Digest*. On evenings such as this, sitting on his front porch in Tennessee with his mother and his aunts, Haley had heard stories about his forebears—especially Kunta Kinte, the one they called the African. Through family stories, he absorbed the tragic struggle and remarkable survival of a people who had been enslaved. At a time when black America was in a struggle for equality, and many African Americans felt the need for a greater sense of identity, Haley—already a writer of distinction and a contributing editor for *Reader's Digest*—wanted to trace his family to its deepest roots, back to his African ancestors.

Not long after the meeting, Haley, a seductive oral storyteller, contacted Mrs. Wallace to tell her he wanted to write a "story-history" of his family. She commissioned Haley to do the research that would create a groundbreaking article for *The Digest*—the first fully realized story of an African American family. She so believed in the project that she agreed to pay his expenses, including travel to Africa. It was quite a commitment. Over the course of ten years, *The Digest* paid Haley the equivalent of $200,000 in today's dollars to trace his family history on three continents, through seven generations. The 688-page book was published in 1976 to rave reviews and ultimately won a Pulitzer Prize.

But this epic work was not without controversy. Haley, who was not a historian, encountered serious obstacles as he tried to piece together years of personal history from oral accounts provided by village elders and others. The stealing of Africans and the lack of written records made sourcing and documentation nearly impossible. In the end, Haley made some regrettable mistakes. He settled a lawsuit, acknowledging that passages had been taken from a novel.

Literary critics and contemporary historians now say Haley's account is flawed, if not fictional in part. But one thing is clear: *Roots* changed the way we think about race in this country and profoundly affected the lives of many people, especially African Americans.

One day in the fall of 1991, 15 years after *Roots* was published and media interest had faded, Haley met his editor, Gary Sledge, at the Chattanooga airport. They were working on a story called "The Man on the Train," included in this volume. Before they could make their way to Haley's car, Haley was stopped three or four times by black people who wanted to greet him, touch him … they almost always wanted to touch him. One young father approached shyly. "Are you Alex Haley?" he asked. "Yes," Haley said. The man began to tear up. "I wish, I wish my son was here. We named him after Kunta Kinte."

The Editors

Contents

Introduction

BY LAWRENCE OTIS GRAHAM

lthough I was an adolescent when Alex Haley's *Roots* was first published in 1976 and considered must-reading, the book had a profound impact on how I came to view my own black identity and the largely nonblack world around me. I had always known that my ancestors were Africans who had been brought as slaves to the American South, but my interest in my family's history had been limited to the 20th-century experiences that my parents and grandparents had endured in their native Memphis, Tennessee.

All of that changed after *Roots* made the bestseller list and the TV miniseries aired. I was fascinated by Haley's ancestors—Kunta Kinte and Kizzy and all the others who struggled and survived through 200 years of history. Suddenly I wanted to better understand where *my* people had come from. Like the rest of the nation—the world, even—I wanted to find the Kunta Kinte in *my* family. I wanted to know the people, the celebrations, the tragedies, the *details* that made my own family's story a unique American experience.

Many of the celebrities featured in this collection offer commentary on what *Roots* means to them—people like Colin Powell, Halle Berry, Ben Vereen, Leslie Uggams, B.B. King. They all acknowledge how Haley's story has enhanced their lives and the lives of their family members.

Alex Palmer Haley, a black man, was born August 11, 1921. Although he and his siblings were raised in the segregated South, outside Memphis, his parents were educated members of the black middle class. His mother was a grammar school teacher and the daughter of a successful businessman who owned a lumber company. His father was a college professor who had earned a master's degree from Cornell University. With this solidly middle-class background, Haley's childhood and adolescence hardly fit the narrow stereotype that all blacks were poor, self-defeating and uneducated.

Perhaps it is because Haley grew up in an intact family of supportive parents and siblings that he chose to focus on the optimism and lessons of triumph and achievement demonstrated by the individuals and communities he profiled during his *Digest* writing career, which spanned nearly four decades, from 1954 to 1991.

By the time he wrote *Roots*, Haley was already well known for his 1960 article, "Mr. Muhammad Speaks," on Muslim leader Elijah Muhammad, considered then "the most powerful black man in America." Out of that article, Haley forged a friendship with Malcolm X, Muhammad's right-hand man. The two men talked several times a week for a year or more. It was Haley who co-authored the controversial bestseller *The Autobiography of Malcolm X*.

Like many of the articles that Haley wrote, including *Roots*, the autobiography touched America's conscience, as it profiled one of our nation's most outspoken black civil rights leaders. It was a book that sat on a nightstand shelf next to my parents' bed throughout the 1960s and early 1970s. The fearless expression of Malcolm's face on the cover stared out at me, almost reminding me that my comfortable existence as a black boy living in an upper-class white neighborhood should not be taken for granted. This fact was richly ironic—or perhaps intentional on my parents' part—because my brother and I were attending the same private grammar school as Malcolm X's daughters, and my mother and his widow, Betty Shabazz, had become close friends, having met at the mostly white PTA meetings.

I grew up with the Shabazz girls, Malcolm's daughters. I saw them at school, played with them at our monthly Jack & Jill (a national black family organization) gatherings, lived in the same Princeton University dormitory with one of them and went to the same black debutante cotillions that were sponsored by our mothers' sorority. I often found myself running back to the pages that Alex Haley had written about their family and their father in particular as I tried to better understand the complexities of this very famous but intensely private family.

This collection of Haley's important works, previously published in *Reader's Digest*, shows us how this one writer was able to introduce us to the richness of the American experience. And it shows us that there is no one narrow definition for being black in America.

In each of the book's four sections, *Stories of Triumph*, *Race and Resilience*, *The Search Begins*, and *The Legacy*, you will clearly see that Haley infused a sense of optimism in all his writings: in the profile of gospel singer Mahalia Jackson ("She Makes a Joyful Music"), who was beloved by the black church community before she became nationally famous for singing "Troubles of the World" during the funeral scene of the Lana Turner movie *Imitation of Life*; in his inspirational story of a teenage high jumper at Boston University ("The Jumpingest Man on Earth") whose foot was crushed in a tragic elevator accident yet who went on to become a medalist in the 1960 Olympics. In every piece, Haley inspires us.

Haley introduces us to his brother in "The Man Who Wouldn't Quit," and we, too, experience the indignities he experienced as one of the first black students to integrate the all-white University of Arkansas School of Law in 1949. While enduring racial taunts and surviving humiliating incidents—human urine was literally thrown at his face by his fellow students—George Haley rose above the prejudice and earned top grades and a place on the prestigious *Law Review*. Haley's father worked his way through college and graduate school as a Pullman porter until he met "The Man on the Train." Always, Haley seems to be telling us, opportunity awaits those who are prepared.

His articles about the Harlem community's struggle to build strong businesses and families in the 1950s ("The Harlem Nobody Knows") and about Olympic track star Wilma Rudolph, who overcame childhood paralysis to become the first American woman to win three Olympic gold medals ("The Girl Who Wouldn't Give Up"), are just as compelling.

One very special feature of this collection is the never-before-published "Aboard the *African Star*," which is edited from a talk Haley gave to Reader's Digest employees in 1991. He spoke candidly about how difficult it was for him to write portions of *Roots*. He explained how, in order to capture the slave-ship experience of his ancestor's voyage from Africa in 1767, he literally sneaked down into the dark hold of a freight ship and lay down on a bare wood plank, where he stowed himself, dressed only in his undershorts.

Traveling from Liberia, Africa, to Florida, he spent ten cold nights, armed with a small flashlight, a pen and a writing pad so that he could record what his ancestors must have felt while crowded together with hundreds of other slaves, some dying or dead, in a dank, unsanitary ship for two months at a time. Haley admits his personal weaknesses as a writer, a professional and as a man. He acknowledges how he struggled to complete *Roots*, a work that took a 12-year toll on him both mentally and physically, and how, deep in debt and behind on his deadlines, he contemplated suicide.

Today Alex Haley's childhood home in Tennessee is included on the National Register of Historic Places and remains an important sightseeing stop for people of all races who recognize how this man taught us to value our family histories. When Haley's funeral took place in Memphis, in February 1992, several of my Memphis relatives attended—not because he had become a national celebrity but because of the pride that he had brought to their community, to our people and to our nation's understanding of American history.

Roots is just as powerful and poignant today as it was when Alex Palmer Haley first wrote it. His greatest gift, as you will see in this rich collection of his work, was the ability to discuss race issues in a way that made two different worlds—one black and one white—accessible to all of us, regardless of our color, our ethnicity, our religion or our age. And he did it in a way that was entertaining, insightful and elegant.

Lawrence Otis Graham, one of the nation's leading experts on race, politics and class in America, is the author of 14 books, including Our Kind of People *and* The Senator and the Socialite, *a biography of the first black to serve a full term in the U.S. Senate.*

Stories of Triumph

Inspiring others to prevail in spite of the odds against them was often a goal behind the profiles that Alex Haley authored. This section looks at two Olympic medalists and an internationally celebrated singer who had to struggle to beat those odds at a time when most could only dream of racial equality. Yet all three of these incredible individuals succeeded by setting a high bar and staying true to themselves and their ideals.

She Makes A Joyful Music

Though tempted by jazz and blues, Mahalia Jackson was born to sing gospel

W hen Mahalia Jackson, the world's greatest gospel singer, walks onstage for a performance, her broad face is radiant under her high, wavy crown of black hair, her lips move soundlessly in the prayer that she will "make a joyful noise unto the Lord," just as her preacher-father always asked her to do in his church.

Then, to soft piano chords, Mahalia intones, "I sing because my soul is happy." Succeeding songs deepen the cathedral hush in the concert hall. Tears glisten on Mahalia's face and add another dimension to the low, rich, impassioned voice. Soon in the packed house many besides Mahalia are weeping.

Abruptly Mahalia shifts to big, jubilant gospels. She booms a tom-tom beat, her eloquently mobile face and large body rejoice in

A radiant Mahalia Jackson belts out jubilant gospels at the Shrine Auditorium in Los Angeles, 1961.

Published in Reader's Digest, November 1961

an exuberant and contagious rhythm. Sophisticated audiences thump their feet and clap hands, shout for a dozen encores.

As she leaves the stage, it's difficult to realize that in the days when Mahalia Jackson was a desperately poor nobody, she had to fight against a recurrent temptation that to anyone else would have been the chance of a lifetime. For most of her life, relatives, friends, musicians, all had wanted her to turn away from her gospel songs to sing jazz and the blues.

In 1915, when Mahalia was four years old, two relatives who were minstrel stars came to her native New Orleans. Mahalia grew up in a tumbledown neighborhood of hardworking Negroes living in shacks near the levee. She began to sing almost as soon as she could walk. The chubby little girl had an unusually "big" voice, and it wasn't long before she could make a congregation shout with the joy of her gospels. After hearing her sing in the small Baptist church pastored by her father, who was a stevedore by day and barber at night, her relatives excitedly offered to teach her minstrel jazz tunes, declaring that she would soon earn enough to turn the poor family rich overnight. Mahalia's mother, however, said, "No! The devil will get no help from this house!"

As the years passed, snatches of all the sounds and rhythms she heard around her crept into the way she sang her gospel—the shouts of the fishermen on the levee, the cries of the washerwomen and roustabouts, the troubles, joys and jazz of a Negro community. Secretly she was flattered when people pointed her out as the girl whose voice could make her another Bessie Smith, the incomparable blues singer. Ambitious to escape her drab girlhood, she walked miles on weekends, to scrub floors for dimes and quarters to help the family income. After finishing eighth grade, she went to work as a laundress. Sometimes, when alone, she would practice singing the Bessie Smith blues songs she heard on other people's gramophones.

But each time Mahalia sang jazz or blues, she was uncomfortable. It wasn't only her mother's objections; it was her own inner feeling that singing gospels was more in keeping with her religious faith. "There was despair in the blues," she has said. "Singing God's music gave me hope."

Mahalia was 17 when an aunt in Chicago sent her an invitation,

Two legends— Nat King Cole and Mahalia Jackson in 1957 on the production set of *St. Louis Blues*.

and a railroad ticket, to visit her. She vowed never to return to New Orleans except in triumph, and promptly found two jobs, as a laundress and as a hotel maid.

Soon after she arrived in Chicago, Mahalia sat riveted by the magnificence of the 50-voice, white-robed choir of the Greater Salem Baptist Church. Immediately after the service, she mustered the courage to ask the choir director to try her out. He invited her to midweek practice.

When practice began that night, she was so nervous that she sang far too loudly for one member of a group. As she became aware of others' eyes on her, her tension increased. But suddenly the director signaled for silence. "Miss Jackson," he asked, "would you try a solo?"

Mahalia began to sing "Hand Me Down My Silver Trumpet, Gabriel." She let the big voice go, singing as uninhibitedly as she had in New Orleans. When she finished, the director and choir members stood gazing at her, open-mouthed. Mahalia was named the Greater Salem Baptist's first soloist.

From her first Sunday as soloist, her transparent reverence hushed the huge congregation—and then the bouncing, revival beat of her gospels drove them to clapping, stomping and shouting their own devotion. Her singing brought her many friends and among them was the man she was to marry—Albert Hockehull, a Tuskegee Institute graduate who worked as a postal clerk because he couldn't find a job in chemistry, for which he was trained.

It was inevitable that Southside Chicago's grapevine would bring

The singer toured the world, packing auditoriums and wowing audiences with her "big" voice and soulful renditions. This studio portrait was taken in 1970.

jazz musicians to hear Mahalia. One Sunday morning, as choir members were donning their robes, an usher rushed in. In the audience was a noted Chicago bandleader. "Sing today, girl," the usher said. "It's your big break!"

Mahalia pictured herself in night clubs, her records playing across the nation. She could send money to her father in New Orleans; she would be able to buy clothes and jewelry. That day she sang her gospels with exuberant beauty. After the service, the bandleader said, "A hundred dollars a week!"

The offer nearly tripled what she was then earning, yet she blurted that she had to think. The bandleader, surprised, gave her his card.

Through the night, Mahalia struggled with aching temptation. But a strong and steady inner voice said that her father was right; she had been given her voice to sing gospels. The glitter of jazz could never replace the glow of singing out her religion. Choir members and others told her she was silly. "There's nothing wrong with jazz," they said. "Our people birthed jazz."

Mahalia suffered the greatest of all her temptations when even her husband wanted her to turn away from gospel singing. In the Depression following 1930, Mahalia and her husband were laid off the same week and joined the legion of people tramping the streets hunting for work.

One night, with only 50 cents for food, she went to audition for a Negro musical, *The Hot Mikado*. She sat through successive singers of popular songs. But when they called her name, she sang "Sometimes I Feel Like a Motherless Child." When she ended, the theater was in a hush, with many people crying. "Right that second, guiltiness swarmed all through me," she says now. She had sung "Motherless Child," but she was applying to sing jazz. Mahalia bolted for the street. She was chosen for the lead role in *Hot Mikado*, but turned it down.

Then Johnny Meyers, a Negro impresario, featured her in a series of gospel concerts. Five thousand people came to the opening performance; as many more milled outside. Meyers suggested that she record a gospel called "I Will Move On Up a Little Higher."

The record sold like wildfire. Negro disk jockeys played it; Negro ministers praised it from their pulpits. When sales passed one million, the Negro press hailed Mahalia Jackson as "the only Negro whom Negroes have made famous." She had come to fame by singing only in Negro communities; few white Americans had even heard of her.

Overnight, Mahalia was deluged with offers from dozens of major Negro figures in jazz. But each of them found a Mahalia who knew where her destiny lay. "God put me here to sing the gospels," she told Louis Armstrong. Replied Armstrong, "You'd be the greatest, but I got to go along with that."

When one of her recordings won a French Academy award, Mahalia consented to a European tour, though she wasn't convinced that foreign audiences would understand the sacred music of her people. But in Paris, Mahalia had 21 curtain calls. When thousands were turned away from her concerts, she doubled her original schedule.

During her rigorous tour, Mahalia became ill. "Once, before a concert," recalls her pianist, "she was too sick to read her Bible as she usually does before going onstage. She asked the manager to read the 98th Psalm, that has in it the verse her daddy used to use: 'Make a joyful noise unto the Lord, all the earth; break forth into joyous song and sing praises!' And when she appeared onstage, her shoulders were thrown back, the usual radiance was on her face. She sang 20 songs and seven encores, and no one suspected how ill she was."

> When finally she closed with "The Lord's Prayer," sung in full, whole, round sounds, the crowd stood breathless.

Back in America, Mahalia moved a packed Madison Square Garden to tears—and roaring applause. In Hollywood, she sang gospels written into two motion pictures for her. She appeared in concerts, made recordings, and guest-starred on TV. On a recent European tour she gave a command performance before the King and Queen of Denmark.

The jazz world has come to Mahalia on her own terms. At the 1958 Newport Jazz Festival, thousands of jazz buffs gave Mahalia's gospel songs a standing ovation. When finally she closed with "The Lord's Prayer," sung not with the usual hushed reverence, but in full, whole, round sounds, the crowd stood breathless. "Mahalia Jackson doesn't *believe* that God exists," wrote one critic. "She *knows* it!"

Today, wherever a Sunday evening finds Mahalia, she finds a church, preferably a little rundown church like her father's, and she may sing until well beyond midnight. "Those humble churches are my filling stations," she says. "If I didn't get in one every time I can, I would run empty." ✦

The Girl Who Wouldn't Give Up

Wilma Rudolph made Olympic history, but even more remarkable is the story behind that victory

Spectators packing Rome's huge Stadio Olimpico last September hushed as the six teams competing in the women's Olympic 400-meter relay final took positions on the track. All eyes were on one girl, the lithe brown 20-year-old who was to run the anchor leg for the U.S. team. Wilma Rudolph, a five-foot-eleven coed from Tennessee State University, had already won the 100- and 200-meter sprints, and in the semifinals of the relay she had played a large part in

Published in Reader's Digest, May 1961

Wilma Rudolph
ran the crucial
anchor leg of the
400-meter relay at
the 1960 Summer
Olympics in
Rome. The team
win gave Rudolph
her third gold
medal.

setting a new Olympic and world record. If the U.S. team won this final, she would be the first American woman ever to win three Olympic gold medals in track.

The starting pistol cracked. The first runners shot from their starting blocks, raced the baton to the second. The second to the third. And now Lucinda Williams of the U.S. team was in the lead, flashing toward Wilma, who had already started her forward motion. Then a gasp went up from the crowd—the baton was bobbled and Wilma had to stop to grasp it! Germany's Jutta Heine was flying two strides ahead. But now Wilma's great, scissoring, incredible strides began to burn up the track. She came abreast of Jutta Heine … pulled slightly ahead … and burst the tape in first place.

A roar went up from 60,000 throats. In the din, one confused spectator had to ask a French photographer standing near the finish line who won. The photographer replied, *"La Gazelle, naturellement. La 'Chattanooga Choo Choo.'"*

Wilma Rudolph's spectacular triumphs at the Olympics brought her tremendous acclaim both at home and abroad. Last December, European sportswriters named her Sportsman of the Year, the first American woman ever so honored. In the United States, she was voted Woman Athlete of the Year. But more remarkable than all the honors is the fact that her triumph was achieved over a staggering handicap: for one third of her life she was a cripple, unable to walk.

A tiny 4½ pounds at birth, Wilma Rudolph was the 17th child in the poor home of a Negro store clerk and a domestic in Clarksville, Tennessee. Always sickly, she was four before she began to toddle. Then she was stricken with scarlet fever and double pneumonia. The child lay near death for weeks. Finally she pulled through, but her left leg had suffered a form of paralysis.

Her mother, a resolute woman, decided that this pitiful child was as deserving of health as the rest. Wrapping Wilma in a blanket, Mrs. Rudolph took her by bus the 45 miles to Nashville's Meharry Medical College. There specialists tested the little girl exhaustively. They said that years of daily therapeutic massage *might* restore the use of the leg. "I can't bring her here every day. Can you teach me?" the mother asked. The doctors could, but there had to be treatment at the clinic also, with special apparatus for heat and water therapy.

She was 5-foot-11, 130 pounds, and lightning fast. Wilma-watchers said, "Don't blink. You might miss her."

For the next two years, Mrs. Rudolph on her weekly day off made the 90-mile round trip to the clinic. The other six days, after arriving home tired from work and preparing the family supper, she carefully massaged the wasted small leg until long after Wilma had fallen asleep. When after a year the doctors could detect only slight improvement in the muscular reflexes, Mrs. Rudolph taught three older children to massage, and there began four daily shifts of "rubbing Wilma." "She's going to walk," Mrs. Rudolph declared.

By 1946 Wilma could manage a sort of hop for short distances, but then the leg would buckle. By the time she was eight she was able to walk with a leg brace. That summer the Meharry clinic substituted a specially reinforced high-top left shoe for the brace, and Wilma limped off happily to school.

ALEX HALEY / THE GIRL WHO WOULDN'T GIVE UP

A brother, Westley, had got a basketball and mounted a peach basket on a pole in the back yard. To the family's surprise, Wilma was soon out on the court, playing basketball almost fanatically. Ignoring the heavy orthopedic shoe, she would swivel and pivot away from Westley, dribble in a weaving crouch, then spring up to make a shot. When others stopped to rest, she would continue alone—"making up," her mother said, "all the playing she'd missed."

One day her mother, returning from work, stood slack-jawed with astonishment: Wilma was bounding around under the peach basket barefoot! She no longer needed the shoe.

Entering Burt High School in 1953, 13-year-old Wilma went out for basketball. Playing with fervor during one game, she collided with Coach Clinton C. Gray, who was refereeing. "You're buzzing around like a skeeter wherever I turn!" he exclaimed, exasperated. "Skeeter" promptly became Wilma's nickname. Not long afterward, Coach Gray inaugurated girls' track. He saw Skeeter run, timed her—and stared at his stop watch in disbelief.

The gangling, unknown Skeeter proved the sensation of the state high-school meet, winning the girls' 50-, 75- and 100-yard dashes. Watching was Edward Stanley Temple, coach of women's track at Tennessee State University. With his crack team of "Tigerbelles," Temple was bent on gaining wider recognition for this Negro university. And in this young girl with the perfect sprinter's body, the long powerful legs and the drive to win, he recognized a potential champion.

Each summer Temple tried out ten high-school-girl track stars; those proving of Tigerbelle caliber could receive a work-aid scholarship for four years at the university. "Be glad to try you out," he told Wilma casually.

The news elated the Rudolph household. "You're the first one in this house that ever had the chance to go to college," Wilma's mother said. "If running's going to do that, I want you to set your mind to be the best! Never give up."

With nine other bobby-soxed speed stars from Negro high schools, Wilma arrived on the Tennessee State campus. Temple promptly let them know this was no picnic. His first order was for a cross-country jog, some five miles across rough farm pastures. Halfway, many of the girls sagged down exhausted, some even retching. Wilma, too, stumbled and fell. But somehow they all dragged themselves back to the track. Temple greeted them bluntly: "If you want to run here, you have to be in condition."

Next morning the girls were routed from bed at 5 a.m. Pairing each candidate with one of his star Tigerbelles, Temple ordered 50-yard sprints. Every high-school runner finished a humiliating five to ten yards behind, and Wilma did worse than most. Back in the dormitory, she cried, sick with shame that she had come. But she thought of her mother saying, "Never give up."

Temple knew exactly how to plant incentive and competitiveness. Relentlessly, he criticized the flaws in her style. "Stretch out those long legs—*stride*! Your elbows look like a windmill. Pump the arms straight, like this. No clenched fists—you run more relaxed with open palms."

He also knew when Wilma reached the point where she was ready to explode. "Look, Skeeter," he said, calming kindness in his voice. "Right now you are a fair runner. But I want great runners. My Tigerbelles make you look bad only because they're better prepared than you. Now you can go home if you want to. Or stay, and I'll teach you how to win races." Pausing, he added, "I think you can be a champion if you want to."

Three days later Wilma was speechless when Temple read her name among the four Junior Tigerbelles he was taking with his college stars to Ponca City, Oklahoma, to participate in National A.A.U. competition. At Ponca City the Junior Division 440-yard relay was won by Temple's four trainees, including Wilma. Their sister Tigerbelles swept all Senior Division sprints and the relay. Tennessee State had its first A.A.U. championship.

Wilma returned to her family and schoolmates a heroine—to everyone but herself. She was still convinced that she could never run as brilliantly as Temple's college girls. Her mother put her finger on the trouble. "It *looks* like you can't," she said, "but you can't think you can't! You just got to forget everything but trying!"

Through the remaining high-school summers, Wilma drilled in the countless details of Tigerbelle style. By the time she was a university freshman Temple was admonishing his summer trainees, "Watch how Rudolph does it." Over and over she would race 100 yards, walk back to the starting line, then race again. She had heard so many starting pistols, counted her early strides so often, that by

> Wilma's mother told her: "You can't think you can't! You just got to forget everything but trying!"

now instinct triggered her catapulting take-offs, told her the exact instant to begin straightening up and "floating" and, seconds later, when to start leaning to meet the tape.

Everywhere they raced, the Tigerbelles demolished the opposition. With the three other members of the relay team—Martha Hudson, Barbara Jones and Lucinda Williams—Wilma ranked as one of Temple's four fastest Tigerbelles. Yet in intrasquad races the other three invariably beat her. "You've got the physical equipment and style; you should be winning. What's wrong?" Temple often asked. She would answer, "I don't know, Coach," for she was trying with all she had.

Then, in November 1959, Wilma began suffering from sore throat, and gradually her tonsils flared into a swelling agony. Temple took her to a Nashville doctor, who performed a tonsillectomy immediately. "Those infected tonsils have been sapping her strength for years," the doctor said.

Three weeks later Wilma returned to the track, in full health for the first time in her life. At the Chicago 1960 Indoor A.A.U. Nationals she blazed to victory in three races. In Corpus Christi she shaved three tenths of a second off the Olympic and world 200-meter record. In the Olympic tryouts at Abilene, Texas, she took the 100 and 200 meters, and anchored the winning Tigerbelle relay team that would represent the United States.

"Somebody will have to set a new world record to beat her in Rome!" Temple exclaimed.

Seven Tigerbelles were among the 310 U.S. athletes who flew to Rome last August. There, in the 100-meter women's sprint, Wilma scorched to a new Olympic record of 11 seconds flat. In the 200-meter trials the following day, she cracked the Olympic standard. Then, in the final, she blazed to breath-stopping victory over Germany's great 200-meter star, Jutta Heine. Not since "Babe" Didrikson's phenomenal performance 28 years before had the United States boasted a woman double gold-medalist.

On the day when her final burst of speed won the relay for the Tigerbelles and made her a triple gold-medalist, a deafening ovation exploded in the Stadio Olimpico. "Wilma!" the crowd roared. "*Gazzella Nera* [Black Gazelle]!" "Skeeter!" Hats, newspapers, programs and autograph books rained down on the emerald-green field as the lean brown girl half-circled and jogged toward the side lines.

"Coach Temple! Coach Temple!" Wilma was crying as athletes and photographers mobbed her. She was the world's Queen of Track, flooding out tears of gratitude for Temple's persevering training, for her mother's determination that a puny, crippled daughter must walk.

Back in the United States, Wilma was so lionized that it was ten days before she could return to a clamorous home town. Clarksville's "Welcome Wilma Day" saw every school and business closed, and the entire population lined up to cheer the champion.

Wilma takes all such adulation in her graceful stride. She has settled quickly again into life at the university. She is continuing to win races, indoors and out. She is majoring in elementary education, preparing for a career of grammar-school teaching and coaching high-school girls' track. In the roles of teacher and coach she will pass on to other youngsters the important lesson she learned: that those who really want to can win. ✦

The Jumpingest

Teen champion John Thomas made one of the most dramatic comebacks in the history of sports

A t Boston University in March 1959, an 18-year-old freshman stepped into an elevator, dropped onto a stool and pushed the handle to go up. He was John Thomas, a lanky Negro youth of 6 feet 5 inches who only a month earlier had set new records with an "impossible" 7-foot-1¼-inch high jump. Track fans considered him America's top bet to win a gold medal in the 1960 Olympics. Now he sat relaxed with his long legs spraddled out. He did not notice that his left foot was sticking out through the metal-grille door of the old-fashioned elevator cage—until suddenly the desert boot he wore was caught between the rising elevator and the next floor. In a split second his foot was mashed.

Torn with anguish and pain, Thomas was rushed to the Massachusetts Memorial Hospitals. Surgeons hastily examined the

Known for his jungle-cat strides, John Thomas stretches until his body cries for rest, then he does more.

Published in Reader's Digest, June 1960

Man on Earth

foot. X rays showed no fractures, but tissue had been lacerated so the tendons of all the toes, and some of the nerves, were exposed. Abrasions made it questionable that the skin would survive. As the surgeons prepared to operate, press wires flashed the news across the United States. To sportswriters and fans everywhere it looked like the end of a fantastic career that had just begun.

No patient in the hospital was calmer than John Thomas. Almost as soon as he was removed from the operating room, his pleasant, triangular face mustered a smile for the nurses. But the cast on his lower left leg made him realize that his athletic future was in doubt. His mother was his first visitor. She saw in his eyes the same quiet determination to win that she had seen so often before. She knew her boy. "You're going to jump again, John," she told him. "Everything's going to work out all right."

To avoid deterioration of his muscles, Thomas, while still in bed, began exercising doggedly on an apparatus of pulleys and weights. Therapists kneaded and massaged the leg above the plaster cast. But then it became apparent that the skin would not survive. The healing process would cause contraction and stiffening of the toes. To prevent this there would have to be a skin graft. On April 27 Dr. Chester W. Howe performed the operation. Skin $\frac{1}{10,000}$ of an inch thick was cut from Thomas's left thigh and sutured with fine silk over the butterfly-shaped wound on his foot.

Finally, in mid-May, Thomas was discharged. His left calf had not shrunk as much as expected, but it was still three quarters of an inch thinner than the right.

As in previous years, he spent the summer at a Boy Scout camp. Boston University athletic officials and doctors agreed it would be all right if he would "take it very easy on that foot." He complied by taking only short walks at first—but the rest of the time he was lifting weights, doing stretching exercises, massaging his calf, swimming. Always he exercised until his body cried for rest, and then he did a little more. Slowly he lengthened the hikes until he was walking long distances without having to stop to ease the injured foot. And in late summer, when he returned to Boston, he displayed the old, elastic stride.

Though football was not his sport, he asked to accompany the university football team to its training camp. There he was soon catching passes with an expertness that made the regular ends unashamedly envious. No one would have pushed him as hard in training as he now drove himself. Said a coach, "To see a champion fighting through—it is a beautiful thing to watch."

Then last January came the sensational announcement: in the Boston Knights of Columbus Meet, first track meet of the 1960 indoor collegiate season, Boston University would enter John Thomas in the high jump.

Applause filled the packed house as Thomas, looking straight ahead, walked toward what B.U. students have called his "launching pad." It was ten months since he had last jumped publicly. Standing alone in white shirt and crimson shorts, he watched an official turn a marker to indicate that the bar was set at a warm-up height of 6 feet 2½ inches. The noise had become a pin-drop hush. Suddenly John Thomas moved… seven lengthening, jungle-cat strides. Then the spikes on the crucial left foot dug in while the right leg lashed up in a mighty high-kick, and he was over the bar with space to spare.

Thomas made four more jumps, with the bar raised two inches each time. Finally the bar rested at 7 feet ½ inch. He cleared it—and the arena exploded into a standing, roaring ovation for a champion's dramatic comeback.

And Thomas had accomplished it calmly and without bravura. "Nothing fazes him," says Vic Stout, B.U. athletic director. "There have been few youngsters in the history of sports who have had so much publicity heaped on their heads. But John has stood up under it beautifully."

At the February 1961 Millrose Games, Thomas prepares to walk toward his "launching pad."

John grew up across the river from Boston, in Cambridge, where his father drives a bus. He was a quiet youngster whose life revolved around sports, Boy Scouting and the youth activities of the Ebenezer Baptist Church. In his senior year at Rindge Technical High School, coached by Tom Duffy, he dominated New England track competition, establishing high-jump records in eight major "schoolboy" meets and also winning the state high-hurdle event. When he graduated in 1958, John was invited to join a group of American trackmen about to compete in Japan.

There, before huge crowds, he jumped in seven meets, and became the Japanese national champion with a prodigious leap of 6 feet 10⅝ inches. He was staggered when teammates pointed out that he had only another five eighths of an inch to go to tie the Olympic record. "It made me realize that I maybe could really do that," John says.

College recruiters from around the country had approached John while he was still in high school. But Boston University was close to home, and John, who wants to be a teacher-coach, could pursue a degree in education there. He chose B.U.

To make his style as nearly faultless as possible, John spends hours in unrelenting practice. The "straddle roll" he uses is described as "stride, gather, kick, bounce, relax and roll." John approaches the bar from the left, his seven loping strides getting longer as he goes, until the last one spans eight and a half feet. Then the left foot brakes him and he springs off that heel, a split second ahead of the powerful right-leg high-kick. Slow-motion films show his body rolling over the bar almost languidly, the left leg following. Then he lands on his buttocks in a pit filled three feet deep with foam-rubber chunks.

Thomas never knows how high he jumps in practice, for then he is thinking only of form and style. His coaches, Doug Raymond and Ed Flanagan, set the bar and he never asks at what level. Last March 11, in an airliner bound for the Chicago Relays, Raymond told him, "John, you did seven-two last Tuesday." "I *did*?" exclaimed Thomas.

That night, thousands saw Thomas go 7 feet 2½ inches, smashing for the fourth time the record he set in 1959. This remains the highest Thomas has ever jumped in public. When his coaches are asked if he has gone higher in practice, they just smile.

Track fans confidently expect that, at the 1960 World Olympics in Rome this August and September, he will lift the crown from the

present titleholder, Charles Dumas of the University of Southern California. The closest other competitor will probably be Russia's outdoor champion, Yuri Stepanov, whose highest leap so far has been 7 feet 1 inch. At Boston University, Olympic confidence is at such a peak that the Varsity Club has already presented a round-trip ticket to Rome to Coach Raymond.

His coaches have an affection for John Thomas that is deep and obvious. "A kid so nice you'd be proud if he was your own," says Raymond. "He has manners and dignity—you can see the mark of the boy who grew up in the Boy Scouts and the church."

Shy to the point of wariness of anyone desiring to make a hero of him, John seems to regard manifestations of his fame with a startled, objective awe. But he sincerely enjoys his steady stream of fan mail from around the world, acknowledging every letter and saving the foreign stamps. Often he is asked in his fan mail about problems he has encountered because of his race. This question embarrasses him. He answers frankly that he has had no such problems.

John's father, making his bus circuit, is constantly responding to queries about his boy or acknowledging congratulations. "I try not to be *too* proud," he says. ◆

John Thomas was only 17 when he became the first man to clear the "impossible" 7-foot indoor barrier in 1959.

GEORGE SILK/TIME LIFE PICTURES/GETTY IMAGES

ALEX HALEY / THE JUMPINGEST MAN ON EARTH

Race and Resilience

On the eve of the landmark 1954 Supreme Court decision *Brown v. Board of Education*, Haley introduced readers around the world to a Harlem community that was thriving, proving that equal opportunity could foster the growth of successful businesses, schools and families. Along with "The Harlem Nobody Knows," this section offers works by Haley that look at three individuals—his father, his brother and Muslim leader Elijah Muhammad—who embodied the idea of challenging racial stereotypes. "Mr. Muhammad Speaks" would lead to Haley's international bestselling book *The Autobiography of Malcolm X*.

The Harlem Nobody Knows

Probably no community on earth has come so far so fast

arlem, the six-square-mile section of New York City where lives the largest concentration of Negroes in the world—375,000—is frequently pointed to as the sinkhole of U.S. capitalism. Here are some of the nation's oldest and most dilapidated buildings. Too many people live in them, too many children crowd the schools. To the colored races who comprise two thirds of the world's population the area is presented by critics as the symbol of American discrimination against the Negro.

These critics of our democracy would do well to take a closer look at the Negroes of Harlem today. Probably no community on earth has come so far so fast.

In this area where hardly a Negro owned property 50 years ago, the collective Negro assessment today approaches 300 million dollars. One bank with four branches in Harlem reports over 20

Photographer Gordon Parks snapped this shot of a boy in Harlem selling newspapers on the street.

GORDON PARKS/FARM SECURITY ADMINISTRATION, OFFICE OF WAR INFORMATION PHOTOGRAPH COLLECTION (LIBRARY OF CONGRESS)

Published in Reader's Digest, June 1954

million dollars in deposits. Negroes operate some 4,300 businesses in Harlem, and 2,200 more elsewhere in New York City. An advertising survey conducted recently reported: "Income of the average Harlem family has tripled since 1940. This community, as an annual market, represents more than a *billion* dollars."

This spectacular progress has all occurred since the turn of the century, when a Negro realtor, Philip A. Payton, persuaded several Harlem landlords to fill vacancies with Negro tenants. A trickle of immigration soon became a tide.

From the first the new community was in economic trouble. Having nothing to sell but unskilled labor, the Negroes suffered from poverty and discrimination. At least half the population was unemployed. Thousands of families escaped the dole only because Harlem's women found jobs as laundresses or household servants.

Conditions improved during World War I, when, because of manpower shortages, hiring taboos were relaxed. Soon Negroes were working in more than 300 occupations. The expanded opportunities gave the area a much-needed financial boost. Hundreds of Harlemites began to make down payments on homes; hundreds more invested in small businesses. In a short time the number of licensed Negro realtors in the city rose from three to 31.

For the most part, however, this spectacular growth went unnoticed by the general public. Instead, Harlem was gaining prominence as a Mecca of Jazz. In the Roaring Twenties its cabarets and dance halls swarmed with revelers.

Then came the depression of 1929. Harlem was hard hit. From the boom-inflated payrolls Negroes were among the first to be fired—by the thousands. The race riots of this era made headlines around the world.

But little notice was taken when the same forces—racial pride and the desperate fight for survival—were subsequently channeled in more disciplined ways to shape Harlem's future. In 1931, for example, the Harlem Businessmen's Club circularized the slogan, "Don't Buy Where You Can't Work!" Negro employees above the level of porter had been rare in Harlem retail stores. When the *Amsterdam News*, Harlem's largest newspaper, threw its power into the campaign, it had the effect of a picket line. In six months Negro clerical and sales help were commonplace.

The New York Urban League prevailed upon officials of government, unions and industry to widen the variety of available jobs. Simultaneously it urged Negroes to develop new skills. By late 1932 Negroes were represented in almost all major occupational groupings—and the Urban League has never relaxed its campaign. In 1953, according to the New York State Commission Against Discrimination, more doors had been opened than there were Negroes qualified to enter. Many of the doors have led to gratifying successes.

Amie Associates, Inc., is a family enterprise begun in 1944 by the brothers William, Errol and Cyril Jones. Starting with $1,600 and some electronics equipment, they rented a loft and solicited Government contracts. By V-J Day they had hired 75 technicians and grossed $200,000 for the design and manufacture of electronic devices for the Navy and Signal Corps, and for subcontracts from Bell Telephone and Western Electric. Now Amie, Inc., is making

June 14, 1938. Lenox Avenue, already the heart of Harlem, is bustling with activity and a booming entrepreneurial spirit.

ALEX HALEY / THE HARLEM NOBODY KNOWS

September 17, 1949. The streets are congested with late-model cars, signs of the economic turnaround.

equipment for the Signal Corps and Robinson Aviation.

Barbara Watson, daughter of a municipal court judge, heads a downtown New York agency of nearly 200 Negro models, serving accounts for nationally advertised products. Olivia Stanford, a YWCA executive, and Rose Morgan, a hair stylist, pooled their savings in 1943, leased a five-story Harlem building and launched "Rose-Meta, House of Beauty." Today they are doing a land-office business, with a second, larger salon in Harlem and branches in Long Island. A total of 302 Rose-Meta employees earn from $55 to $200 weekly.

In 1938 Jimmie Adams got a job as shipping clerk in a downtown camera store; in 1951 he became its manager; this year he and two friends raised $20,000 and opened a store of their own. Roy Mills started as a porter for a sportswear firm; today he is its national distribution manager. Louise Varona, a Hunter College graduate, has built a restaurant-supply business into a $140,000 gross.

A group of Negro physicians and businessmen in 1948 pooled $57,000 to take over a vacant building and equip it as the 55-bed Mt. Morris Park Hospital. That same year another team of Harlem business and professional people opened the first Negro bank in New York State—the Carver Federal Savings and Loan Association. Last December the bank marked its fifth anniversary, with savings accounts totaling three million dollars.

Achievements like these have been repeated many times in Harlem. Today, 96 percent of the employable men and women are working. More than 60 percent of Harlem families have reached the $2,000-$5,000 income level; eight percent have incomes above $5,000 a year. As recently as 20 years ago such levels would have been considered hopelessly unattainable. The 15 percent that earns $1,500 or less about matches the national average.

Harlem's housing conditions are still a problem. During World

NICHOLS/PHOTOGRAPHS AND PRINTS DIVISION, SCHOMBURG CENTER FOR RESEARCH IN BLACK CULTURE, THE NEW YORK PUBLIC LIBRARY, ASTOR, LENOX AND TILDEN FOUNDATIONS

War II one of Harlem's blocks was found to be accommodating 3,781 people. At this density the population of the United States could live in half the area of Greater New York City.

The situation is improving, however. Since 1937 nine housing projects, representing 14,127 apartments, have been occupied or are under construction. At this writing private investors have city authorization and FHA aid to clear 24 slum acres and build two more projects, costing 30 million dollars. They will contain 2,200 apartments renting at $25 per room per month.

Many of the social corrosions that plague Harlem will dwindle as its congestion is relieved. Gangs and delinquency are already under steady attack by powerful guidance and corrective agencies. One of the largest of these is Manhattanville Neighborhood Center, Inc., which functions in a teeming area of West Harlem. In its ten years of existence the Center has established a day-care branch for children of working mothers and prodded city construction of a public-health center. Sites for three housing projects in Manhattanville are now being cleared.

Public schools and churches continue the pattern of progress. P.S. 133, for instance, serves so many pupils that classes must be held in shifts, yet it is considered one of the top five elementary schools in the city. Overall, more Harlem youth are enrolled in high schools today than at any point in history. And ten times as many are in college as in 1940. Harlem now contains nearly 400 churches, including missions, whose total replacement value has been estimated at 21 million dollars.

Edward S. Lewis, executive director of the Urban League of Greater New York and one of Harlem's most esteemed citizens, says: "We still face obstacles, but through the efforts of many we see them dwindling. One of our major difficulties is that in too many minds the Negro remains a problem."

Times are changing. On December 31, 1953, Hulan Edwin Jack, a Harlem Negro, who had risen from stockboy to vice-president of a manufacturing firm, was sworn into office as president of New York City's Borough of Manhattan—the center of metropolitan business and industry, the richest island in the world, where Negroes are outnumbered five to one.

Such changes occurred in New York City, in America, in 50 years. ✦

P.S. 133 serves so many pupils, classes are held in shifts, yet it is considered one of the top five elementary schools in the city.

The Man Who Wouldn't Quit

George Haley was in law school for more than an education

I n low tones the dean was explaining to a prospective law student the conduct expected of him. "We have fixed up a room in the basement for you to stay in between classes. You are not to wander about the campus. Books will be sent down to you from the law library. Bring sandwiches and eat lunch in your room. Always enter and leave the university by the back route I have traced on this map."

The dean felt no hostility toward this young man; along with the majority of the faculty and trustees, he approved the admission of 24-year-old George Haley to the University of Arkansas School of Law. But it was 1949, and this young U.S. Air Force veteran was a Negro. The dean stressed that the key to avoiding violence in this Southern school was maximum isolation.

George was dismayed at the pattern of life laid out for him. He

Young toughs harass a civil-rights worker during the 1963 Mississippi Freedom Walk.

BRUCE DAVIDSON/MAGNUM

Published in Reader's Digest, March 1963

might have entered Harvard Law School, where he would not have had to live the life of a pariah. Yet he had chosen this!

A letter from his father had determined him. During his last semester at Morehouse College in Atlanta he had opened the letter to read: "Segregation won't end until we open beachheads wherever it exists. The governor of Arkansas and educational officials have decided upon a quiet tryout of university integration. You have the needed scholastic record and temperament, and I understand that Arkansas has one of the South's best law schools. I can arrange your admission if you accept this challenge."

George had great love and respect for his father, a college professor and pioneer in Negro education. He accepted the challenge.

The first day of school he went quickly to his basement room, put his sandwich on the table and started upstairs for his class. He found himself moving through wave upon wave of white faces that all mirrored the same emotions— shock, disbelief, then choking, inarticulate rage.

The lecture room was buzzing with conversation, but as he stepped through the door there was silence. He looked for his seat. It was on the side between the other students and the instructor. When the lecture began he tried desperately to concentrate on what the professor was saying, but the hate in that room seeped into his consciousness and obliterated thought.

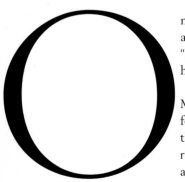

On the second day he was greeted with open taunts and threats: "You nigger, what are you doing here?" "Hey, nigger, go back to Africa." He tried not to hear; to walk with an even pace, with dignity.

The students devised new ways to harass him. Mornings when he came to his basement room he found obscene and threatening notes shoved under the door. The trips from the campus back to his rented room in town became a test of nerve. One afternoon, at an intersection, a car full of students slowed down and waved him across. But the moment he stepped in front of the car they gunned the engine, making him scramble back and fall to his hands and knees in the gutter. As the car sped away he heard mocking laughter and the shouted taunt, "Hey, missing link, why don't you walk on your hind legs?"

His basement room was near the editorial offices of the *Law Review*, a publication written and edited by the 12 top honor men of the senior class. He had heard of their bitterness that he had to share their toilet. One afternoon his door flew open and he whirled to catch in the face a paper bag of urine. After this incident he was offered a key to the faculty toilet; he refused it. Instead, he denied himself liquids during the day and used no toilet.

He began to worry that his passive acceptance of degrading treatment might be destroying him, killing something of his manhood. Wouldn't it be better for him to hate back, to fight back? He took his problems to his father and brother in long, agonized letters.

His father answered, "Always remember that they act the way they do out of fear. They are afraid that your presence at the university will somehow hurt it, and thus hurt their own education and chance in life. Be patient with them. Give them a chance to know you and to understand that you are no threat."

The day after this letter arrived, George found a noose dangling from the ceiling in his basement room.

His brother wrote, "I know it is hard, but try to remember that all our people are with you in thought and prayer."

> The day after the letter arrived, George found a noose dangling from the ceiling in his basement room.

George read this with a wry smile. He wondered what his brother would say if he knew how the town Negroes uneasily avoided him. They knew he walked the thin edge of violence, and they didn't want to be near if an explosion occurred. Only a few gave him encouragement. A church deacon proffered a rumpled dollar bill to help with expenses, saying, "I work nights, son. Walkin' home I see your studyin' light."

Despite his "studyin' light" George barely passed the first-semester exams. His trouble was that in class he couldn't really think; all his nerve endings were alert to the hate that surrounded him. So, the second semester, using a semi-shorthand he had learned in the Air Force, he laboriously recorded every word his professors said. Then at night he blotted out the day's harassments and studied the lectures until he could almost recite them.

By the end of the year George had lost 30 pounds and he went into the examinations exhausted, both physically and emotionally. Somehow he finished them without collapsing, but he had flunked, he thought. He had done his best, and now he could honorably leave. Some other Negro would have to do what he had failed to do, some other man stronger and smarter.

The afternoon the marks were due, heavy with a sense of failure, he went to his basement room, dropped into the chair and put his head on the table. There was a knock on his door and he called, "Come in!" He could hardly believe what he saw. Into the room filed four of his classmates, smiling at him. One said, "The marks were just posted and you made the highest A. We thought you'd want to know." Then, embarrassed, they backed out of the room.

For a moment he was stunned, but then a turmoil of emotion flooded through him. Mostly he felt relief that he didn't have to report failure to his father and friends.

When George Haley returned for his second year at Arkansas there was a sharp decrease in the hate mail under his door, and there was a grudging respect for his scholastic accomplishments. But still, wherever he went, eyes looked at him as if he were a creature from a zoo.

One day a letter arrived: "We are having a 'Race Relations Sunday' and would enjoy having you join our discussion." It was signed by the secretary of the Westminster Presbyterian Student Foundation.

His first reaction was anger. They wanted to *discuss*, did they? Where had these do-gooders been all the time he'd been going through hell? Bitterly he tore up the invitation and threw it in the wastebasket. But that night he tossed restlessly. At last he got out of bed and wrote an acceptance.

At the church, he was met by a group of young men and women. There were the too-hasty handclasps and the too-bright smiles. At last the chairman stood up to introduce George. He said, "We hope that Mr. Haley will tell us what we can do as a Christian body …"

George got to his feet and moved stonily to the podium. Those introductory words released something deep in his maelstrom of emotions. He forgot his carefully prepared speech. "What can you do?" he blurted out. "You can *speak* to me!"

Suddenly, all that had been dammed up came pouring out. He told them what it was like to be treated like an enemy in your own country; what it did to the spirit to be hounded for no crime save that of skin color; what it did to the soul to begin to believe that Christ's teachings had no validity in this world. "I've begun to hate," he confessed. "I've drawn on every spiritual resource I have to fight off this hatred, but I'm failing."

Suddenly his eyes flooded with tears of anger, then of shame. He groped for his chair.

The silence vanished in a roar of applause and cheers. When the chairman's gavel finally restored order, George was unanimously voted a member of the group. Thereafter he spent a part of each weekend at Westminster House, enjoying the simple pleasure of human companionship.

A slight thaw also began to take place at the university. George's classmates gingerly began moments of shoptalk with him, discussing cases. One day he overheard a group discussing a legal point, and one of them said, "Let's go down and ask Haley in the Noose Room." He knew only a moment of indignation—then he smiled! It was an important change.

Toward the end of his second year a senior asked, with elaborate casualness, why didn't he write some articles for the *Law Review*. It was traditional that only the best students received such invitations, and he felt himself flushing with pride.

It was only after he returned to school for his third and final year that he decided to go to the cafeteria. He didn't really want to go. In this last year he longed to relax, to let down his guard. But he was in this school for more than an education.

He went and stood in the cafeteria line. The other students moved away from him in both directions so that he moved in his

In 1948, after a federal court ruling forced the University of Oklahoma to accept him, George McLaurin, a retired professor, sits apart from the other students.

own private air space. His tray was almost loaded when three hulking students ahead shouted, "Want to eat with us, nigger?"

They jostled him, knocking his tray to the floor with a clatter of breaking dishes. As George stooped to retrieve it, his eyes blazed up at his tormentors and for the first time he shouted back. "You're adults!" he said. "Grow up!" They shrank from him in mock terror.

Shaking, George replaced the dumped food and made his way to a vacant table. He bent his head over the crockery. Suddenly a balding, angular student stopped beside him with his tray and drawled, "My name is Miller Williams. Mind if I sit here?" George nodded. Now the two of them were the center of all eyes. Now the taunts were directed at the white student, the words "nigger lover."

Miller Williams was hardly that. "I was born in Hoxie, Arkansas," he said, "and have spent all my life in the South. But what's happening here just isn't right, and I'm taking my stand with you."

Later that day Williams brought several students to George's room for a bull session, and they laid it on the line. "Don't all you niggers carry knives?" George emptied his pockets—no knife. "How often do you bathe?" Every day, George told him. "Don't most of you lust after white girls?" George showed him snapshots of a pretty Negro girl he was dating in his hometown.

Following this session he wrote his brother, "Improving race relations is at least 50 percent a matter of simple communication. Now that I'm able to talk to a few whites I realize what terrible beliefs cause their prejudice. I can see the emotional struggle they are going through just to see me as an equal human being."

Increasingly the last year became a time of triumph, not only for George but for the white students who were able to discard their own preconceptions. When a student sidled up to him and said, "I wrote you a letter I'm sorry for," George stuck out his hand and the student shook it. When another silently offered him a cigarette, George, who didn't smoke, puffed away, knowing it was far more than a gesture.

He was named to the *Law Review* staff, and his writing won an award from the Arkansas Law Review Corp. His winning paper represented the university in a national competition. The faculty chose him as a moot-court defense attorney, and his *Law Review* colleagues picked him as comments editor—the man entrusted with the selection of articles to print.

School was drawing to a close and he felt a deep satisfaction in having accomplished most of his goals. But then the old specter rose again. Each year distinguished alumni returned for a faculty banquet to salute the *Law Review* staff. With a sinking feeling George dreaded what would happen. And that evening when he entered the hotel banquet hall the reaction was just what he had feared. The moment the alumni saw him, a pall fell on the room.

George felt sick. The food passed his lips untasted. It came time for speeches. The law-school dean, Robert A. Leflar, welcomed the alumni and introduced the student editors, one at a time. There seemed an eternity of names and George felt a frozen smile on his face.

Dean Leflar said, "The next young man demands, and receives, as much if not more respect than any other person in our law school."

Suddenly 11 chairs scraped back, and 11 men stood up. They were the *Law Review* editors, and they were looking at George and applauding vigorously. Then the faculty stood up and added cheers to the applause. Finally the old grads got up, the judges and lawyers and politicians from the Deep South, and the ovation became thunderous. "Speech! Speech!" they shouted.

> "I've spent all my life in the South, but what's happening here just isn't right. I'm taking my stand with you."

George Haley pushed himself to his feet. He could say no word for he was unashamedly crying. But that was a kind of speech, too.

Today, ten years later, George is a respected lawyer in Kansas City, Kansas. He has been deputy city attorney since 1955. He is a steward in his church, has helped found a number of Negro business firms and is vice president of the state Young Republicans.

Dozens of his old schoolmates are now George's close friends, but perhaps the most touching acceptance of him as a man came a few years ago when he received a telephone call from Miller Williams, who had sat with him in the cafeteria. Miller, now an instructor of English at Louisiana State University, called to announce the birth of a daughter. "Lucy and I were wondering," he said, "whether you'd care to be her godfather?"

This simple request made forever real the love and respect between two people. George knew that the long struggle and pain had been worthwhile. He knew, too, that his father had been right in saying, "Be patient with them. Give them a chance to know you."

I know it, too. For I am George's brother. ✦

ALEX HALEY / THE MAN WHO WOULDN'T QUIT

Mr. Muhammad Speaks

As head of a fast-growing, anti-white, anti-Christian cult, this mild-looking man is considered "the most powerful black man in America"

A s another Negro and I walked down the main hall of the New York City Public Library, a third, a stranger, joined us. He apologized, "I couldn't help overhearing that you were discussing Mr. Muhammad. It seems that whenever I notice two of us talking, he's the subject."

I had recently arrived from San Francisco. There, too, Negroes were talking about the small, light-brown man who calls himself "Elijah Muhammad, the Messenger of Allah to the Lost-Found Nation of Islam in North America." The founder and leader of a vitriolically anti-white, anti-Christian cult that preaches black superiority, Muhammad bluntly declares, "I am doing all I can to make the so-called Negroes see that the white race and its religion, Christianity, are their open enemies."

Elijah Muhammad, founder of The Nation of Islam, in his trademark kufi hat.

Published in Reader's Digest, March 1960

With a program built on tenets allegedly taught to him by "Almighty God Allah in Person," Muhammad has converted to his "Muslim"—cult pronunciation, *moose'lem*—religion an estimated 70,000 Negroes. (These should not be confused with the 33,000 true Moslems in America.) He has established over 50 "Temples of Islam" and numerous smaller missions that operate in rented quarters or private homes, in 27 states—north and south, and coast to coast. The largest are in Chicago, Detroit and New York; the fastest-growing, in Los Angeles, Atlanta and Miami. In addition, there are in Chicago and Detroit two "Universities of Islam"—the latter accredited through ninth grade—where "Future Leaders of Islam" attend classes 50 weeks a year, and third-graders start learning Arabic.

In an effort to eliminate Negro dependence on whites, Muhammad promotes Muslim-owned and patronized businesses: dress shops, barbershops, groceries, dry cleaners, restaurants, bakeries, a department store, apartment buildings. Now in the financing stage is a Chicago "Islamic Center," which will cover two city blocks and cost 20 million dollars.

His appeal seems to be chiefly among the great masses of Negroes who have migrated to large cities and have been unable to acquire satisfactory new identities. To these, he offers a new way of life—a militant and arrogant black unity. "This is a fast-growing form of black fascism," says Father William McPeak of All Saints' Parish, Harlem. Dr. J. Oscar Lee, of the National Council of Churches, says, "The doctrine used is most dangerous. But we are forced to concede that its followers get a new pride and purpose."

When I went to hear Mr. Muhammad, New York's 5,000-seat St. Nicholas Arena was packed. The floor was lined with standees; 1,000 of the faithful were in the basement and many more were outside. They would hear the message on loudspeakers.

The meeting was opened by Wallace D. Muhammad, one of Muhammad's six sons. Next to speak was Muhammad's tall, whip-smart assistant, a New York minister named "Malcolm X." He

had been serving a sentence for larceny in the Charlestown, Massachusetts, state prison when he was converted.

"When I was a Christian I was a criminal. I was only doing what the white man taught me," Malcolm X was saying calmly, conversationally.

Suddenly, shouting rose from the audience. From the rear marched two double rows of Muslim men. Between them walked a meek-looking little man wearing a blue suit and an embroidered pillbox fez.

Malcolm X waved furiously to stop the wild ovation. Then he introduced the shy-looking little man as "the *boldest* black man in America … the most *powerful* black man in America … the *smartest* black man in America."

Muhammad took the rostrum. For two hours he shouted such statements as: "Everybody has failed the Negro! … Christianity has failed! … the FBI has failed! Christianity is a white man's religion! It contains no salvation for the black man! … Properly read, the Resurrection means that we, the black men of North America, will rise from mental death—then, like Joseph, go on to become master

Elijah Muhammad introduces Malcolm X, his whip-smart aide-de-camp, at a lecture in Chicago on February 26, 1961.

ALEX HALEY / MR. MUHAMMAD SPEAKS

in the land wherein we once were slaves. … Why, after 400 years of murder, rape and slavery, do our oppressors now wave the olive branch of integration? Our oppressors are determined to keep our eyes in the sky while they control the land under our feet—smite our cheeks, rob our pockets! … They do not *want* a united Negro! They do not *want* an Islamic Negro! They know that Islam frees black men from fear!"

Afterward, Muhammad's words were discussed throughout Harlem—in apartments, along the sidewalks, in taverns and restaurants. Exclaimed a retired U. S. Coast Guard steward: "What kind of fools sit and hear him run down God?" A social worker at her desk: "The man is either a gifted opportunist or a psychotic!"

But for every antagonist, at least three defended Muhammad. For example, a woman in a beauty parlor said, "Muhammad just talks facts, and white people call it hate. Negroes already got plenty to hate—he's just bringing it out! If they want to stop Muhammad, the quickest way is to stop the Faubuses."

"It's got to go further than that," said another. "Integrate schools—what have you got? Graduation day, white kids go in one direction, and black another. They know better than to ask for the jobs the white kids get. The Constitution says the same thing for all the citizens—it just gets twisted when it's us!"

And still another: "You read where some of them Southern churches fire preachers for just *talking* tolerance. Sunday morning is the most Jim Crow day in this country. It's going to be a bad time in heaven, I think."

None of it was surprising to a professor of sociology, who said, "I've studied this man. He would never have got off the ground without so many evils to point out. But Muhammad's the extravaganza. Go to a routine temple meeting if you want to see the real spadework."

I went to Harlem's Temple of Islam No. 7, the next Sunday afternoon. Facing us there was a blackboard; painted on it was an American flag, captioned "Slavery, Suffering, Death"; opposite it was an Islamic Star and Crescent, captioned "Freedom, Justice, Equality." Printed between the two was, "Which One Will Survive the War of Armageddon?" After an inflammatory harangue by a 26-year-old

Korean War veteran named "Curtis 2-X," all non-Muslims were invited to step to the rear of the temple to declare themselves.

All new converts begin a series of intensive lectures and lessons. The core of these is fierce black-race pride: "You are superior. Act it." "Principles of Belief in Islam" come next: keep up prayer; spend of what Allah has given in the cause of truth; speak truth despite circumstances; keep clean internally and externally; love the brother or sister believer as oneself; be kind; kill no one whom Allah has not ordered to be killed; worship no God but Allah; fear no one but Allah; never be the aggressor, but always defend yourself if attacked.

In other edicts that alter personal habits, Muhammad prompts even his severest critics to agree when he says he attacks "traditional reasons the Negro race is weak." Alcohol, tobacco, drugs are banned, along with swearing, gambling and dancing. A Muslim woman may not use cosmetics; she may never be alone in a room with any man but her husband. Old friends of new Muslims are astounded at the incredible changes of personality which take place as converts swap lifelong habits for new spartan standards.

> "I've studied this man. He would never have got off the ground without so many evils to point out."

Adult Muslims attend classes one night a week. Men take "physical hygiene"—body-building, military drilling and judo. Selected students between 18 and 30 compose the elite corps, "Fruit of Islam," who travel in chartered buses to wherever Muhammad speaks.

"It's nothing more than you find in the YMCA, CYO, Masons or Boy Scouts," New York minister Malcolm X said of "physical hygiene." But law-enforcement officials view it differently. New York City deputy police commissioner Walter Arm points out that in emotionally tense minority communities, a Muslim interpretation of "defend yourself," backed by the well-trained "Fruit of Islam," could easily ignite a riot.

I applied through Malcolm X to interview the leader, and flew to Chicago to be available when his heavy schedule would permit an appointment. Elijah Muhammad had come a long way from Sandersville, Georgia, where, in October 1897, he was christened Elijah Poole, the son of a Baptist minister.

After an eighth-grade education, Elijah moved to Detroit where, he says, he met "Allah in Person" in 1931. This was a man named Fard Muhammad—"the first and only man born in Mecca who came to America for the express purpose of teaching the so-called Negro."

Fard Muhammad allegedly tutored Elijah, who then founded the first Temple of Islam, in Detroit. Moving later to Chicago, Elijah was arrested for lecturing against Negroes' fighting "the white man's war." Absolved of sedition but found guilty of draft-dodging, he served three years in the Federal Correction Institution at Milan, Michigan.

Released in 1946, he concentrated on grooming dedicated assistants. The staff has at its core Muhammad's six sons. A son-in-law, 210-pound Raymond Sharrieff, is "Supreme Captain" of the "Fruit of Islam." Malcolm X is an ubiquitous aide-de-camp who flies about the United States counseling city and territorial ministers, who in turn designate subordinate lieutenants, sergeants and corporals within the congregation. This deep-rooted organization gives Elijah Muhammad a control and direct power unequaled among Negro leaders.

Nowhere is the Muslim bond of unity displayed more graphically than in their business establishments, which do brisk trade. But Muslim cash registers provide only part of the revenue that reaches Muhammad. At the St. Nicholas Arena in New York I saw no coins in the offering—nothing but bills fluttered into the large paper sacks which ushers passed in the packed hall. More money comes from monthly bazaars and sidewalk sales of jellies, pies, candies and cakes.

All together, enough U.S. Negro dollars flow in to Mr. Muhammad to enable him to finance new businesses, amass funds to begin the $20 million Center and purchase a large, modern Chicago apartment building. (From the latter he evicted white tenants, moved in Negroes, then lowered the rent—a point not lost upon non-Muslim Negroes.)

A few days after the interview I was invited to dine with the Muhammad family. Muhammad spoke in a calm voice—mostly of his problems. The FBI, for instance, was building a thickening file on the organization's activities. He knew that a Congressional probe was rumored, and that the Internal Revenue Service maintains keen interest in Muslim finance. But he said that he fears no agencies. "I have all I need—the truth," he said.

Five times during dinner, Mr. Muhammad excused himself to take long-distance calls. As the evening waned, he occasionally gave a glimpse of his dreams. "What 20 million Negroes could finance for themselves with just a dollar apiece a month!" he once exclaimed. Again, he mused, "— a million black people under the Crescent …"

Among every 300 Negroes there is one registered Muslim—anti-white, anti-Christian, resentful, militant, disciplined—and sworn to follow Elijah Muhammad to the death. How far can he go?

In Chicago, Detroit, Washington, Philadelphia and New York, I talked with top-caliber Negro professional men, with scholars and executives to whom the mere thought of cult membership is repugnant. I heard unanimous denunciation of the anti-white, anti-Christian aspects of the Muslim program. Yet all these people felt that beyond doubt Muhammad is a figure to be reckoned with—because there is so much truth in his charges.

As long as inequity persists in our democratic system, Elijah Muhammad—or some variation of him—will be able to solicit among the Negro population enough followers to justify the title, "the most powerful black man in America." It is important for Christianity and democracy to help remove the Negroes' honest grievances and thus eliminate the appeal of such a potent racist cult. ✦

The Man on the Train

His investment paid dividends he could not have imagined

Whenever my brothers, sister and I get together we inevitably talk about Dad. We all owe our success in life to him—and to a mysterious man he met one night on a train.

Our father, Simon Alexander Haley, was born in 1892 and reared in the small farming town of Savannah, Tennessee. He was the eighth child of Alec Haley—a tough-willed former slave and part-time sharecropper—and of a woman named Queen.

Although sensitive and emotional, my grand-

Published in Reader's Digest, February 1991

mother could be tough-willed herself, especially when it came to her children. One of her ambitions was that my father be educated.

Back then in Savannah a boy was considered "wasted" if he remained in school after he was big enough to do farm work. So when my father reached the sixth grade, Queen began massaging Grandfather's ego.

"Since we have eight children," she would argue, "wouldn't it be prestigious if we deliberately *wasted* one and got him educated?" After many arguments, Grandfather let Dad finish the eighth grade. Still, he had to work in the fields after school.

But Queen was not satisfied. As eighth grade ended, she began planting seeds, saying Grandfather's image would reach new heights if their son went to high school.

Her barrage worked. Stern old Alec Haley handed my father five hard-earned ten-dollar bills, told him never to ask for more and sent him off to high school. Traveling first by mule cart and then by train—the first train he had ever seen—Dad finally alighted in Jackson, Tennessee, where he enrolled in the preparatory department of Lane College. The black Methodist school offered courses up through junior college.

Dad's $50 was soon used up, and to continue in school, he worked as a waiter, a handyman and a helper at a school for wayward boys. And when winter came, he'd arise at 4 a.m., go into prosperous white families' homes and make fires so the residents would awaken in comfort.

Poor Simon became something of a campus joke with his one pair of pants and shoes, and his droopy eyes. Often he was found asleep with a textbook fallen into his lap.

The constant struggle to earn money took its toll. Dad's grades began to founder. But he pushed onward and completed senior high. Next he enrolled in A & T College in Greensboro, North Carolina, a land-grant school where he struggled through freshman and sophomore years.

One bleak afternoon at the close of his second year, Dad was called into a teacher's office and told that he'd failed a course—one that required a textbook he'd been too poor to buy.

A ponderous sense of defeat descended upon him. For years he'd given his utmost, and now he felt he had accomplished nothing. Maybe he should return home to his original destiny of sharecropping.

But days later, a letter came from the Pullman Company saying he was one of 24 black college men selected from hundreds of applicants to be summertime sleeping-car porters. Dad was ecstatic. Here was a chance! He eagerly reported for duty and was assigned a Buffalo-to-Pittsburgh train.

The train was racketing along one morning at about 2 a.m. when the porter's buzzer sounded. Dad sprang up, jerked on his white jacket and made his way to the passenger berths. There a distinguished-looking man said he and his wife were having trouble sleeping, and they both wanted glasses of warm milk. Dad brought milk and napkins on a silver tray. The man handed one glass through the lower-berth curtains to his wife and, sipping from his own glass, began to engage Dad in conversation.

Pullman Company rules strictly prohibited any conversation beyond "Yes, sir" or "No, ma'am," but this passenger kept asking questions. He even followed Dad back into the porter's cubicle.

A Pullman porter and member of the Brotherhood of Sleeping Car Porters, the first African American union to sign a collective bargaining agreement with a major U.S. corporation.

"Where are you from?"

"Savannah, Tennessee, sir."

"You speak quite well."

"Thank you, sir."

"What work did you do before this?"

"I'm a student at A & T College in Greensboro, sir." Dad felt no need to add that he was considering returning home to sharecrop.

The man looked at him keenly, finally wished him well and returned to his bunk.

The next morning, the train reached Pittsburgh. At a time when 50 cents was a good tip, the man gave five dollars to Simon Haley, who was profusely grateful. All summer, he had been saving every tip he received, and when the job finally ended, he had accumulated

Slaves helped build the rail lines that would ultimately provide new employment opportunities for freed blacks.

enough to buy his own mule and plow. But he realized his savings could also pay for one full semester at A & T without his having to work a single odd job.

Dad decided he deserved at least one semester free of outside work. Only that way would he know what grades he could truly achieve.

He returned to Greensboro. But no sooner did he arrive on campus than he was summoned by the college president. Dad was full of apprehension as he seated himself before the great man.

"I have a letter here, Simon," the president said.

"Yes, sir."

"You were a porter for Pullman this summer?"

"Yes, sir."

"Did you meet a certain man one night and bring him warm milk?"

"Yes, sir."

"Well, his name is Mr. R. S. M. Boyce, and he's a retired executive of the Curtis Publishing Company, which publishes *The Saturday Evening Post.* He has donated $500 for your board, tuition and books for the entire school year."

My father was astonished.

The surprise grant not only enabled Dad to finish A & T, but to graduate first in his class. And that achievement earned him a full scholarship to Cornell University in Ithaca, New York.

In 1920, Dad, then a newlywed, moved to Ithaca with his bride, Bertha. He entered Cornell to pursue his Master's degree, and my mother enrolled at the Ithaca Conservatory of Music to study piano. I was born the following year.

One day decades later, editors of *The Saturday Evening Post* invited me to their editorial offices in New York to discuss the condensation of my first book, *The Autobiography of Malcolm X.* I was so proud, so happy, to be sitting in those wood-paneled offices on Lexington Avenue. Suddenly I remembered Mr. Boyce, and how it was his generosity that enabled me to be there amid those editors, as a writer. And then I began to cry. I just couldn't help it.

We children of Simon Haley often reflect on Mr. Boyce and his investment in a less fortunate human being. By the ripple effect of his generosity, we also benefited. Instead of being raised on a sharecrop farm, we grew up in a home with educated parents, shelves full of books, and with pride in ourselves. My brother George is chairman of the U.S. Postal Rate Commission; Julius is an architect, Lois a music teacher and I'm a writer.

Mr. R. S. M. Boyce dropped like a blessing into my father's life. What some may see as a chance encounter, I see as the working of a mysterious power for good.

And I believe that each person blessed with success has an obligation to return part of that blessing. We must all live and act like the man on the train. ✦

The Search Begins

Although much of *Roots* takes place in the 19th century, Haley's literary career was heavily shaped during the 1960s, '70s and '80s, when African Americans and others developed a greater curiosity about their own family histories. Haley talks in this section about the path he took to trace his roots, beginning on a porch in Henning, Tennessee. That journey into the past led him to the story of how the hymn "Amazing Grace" came to be written by a former slave-ship captain. In "The Shadowland of Dreams" he's tempted to give up on his writing. But it is in the never-before-published "Aboard the *African Star*" that Haley tells of his personal struggles against financial ruin, his thoughts of suicide, and his eventual success as a writer and social historian.

The Amazing Grace of John Newton

In London on July 24, 1725, John Newton was born to a pious and shy mother and an authoritarian father. To the boy's relief, his shipmaster father would spend only a few weeks at home between year-long voyages.

When John was seven, his mother died of tuberculosis. The shipmaster, practical man that he was, remarried before his next voyage; for John, however, the loss of his mother was devastating. He became stubborn, disrespectful and difficult, and soon was packed off to a boarding school.

There he was confronted with a headmaster who wielded a cane and a birch rod. The experience "almost broke my spirit," he later confided in a letter. But more torment was in store.

At age 11, John was put to sea as an apprentice sailor on his father's ship. During this time he strayed further and further from his mother's religious teachings.

Captives being brought on board a slave ship lying off Africa's west coast.

Published in Reader's Digest, October 1986
ANN RONAN PICTURE LIBRARY/HERITAGE IMAGES/THE IMAGE WORKS

John Newton, once a British slave-ship captain, helped inspire the abolition of slavery. He wrote "Amazing Grace," the hymn that is "a personal testament to salvation."

By his teens, he was an expert sailor, but his father apprenticed him to a merchant at Alicante, Spain. The 15-year-old disobeyed orders, fought with anyone who crossed him, and was sent back because of his unsettled behavior. As he later confessed, "I believe for some years I never was an hour in any company without attempting to corrupt them."

Next his father arranged for John to learn the plantation business in Jamaica. Before leaving, the youth went to visit his mother's relatives in Chatham, England, and, in one of the twists of circumstance that filled Newton's life, met and fell in love with Mary Catlett, not quite 14. Mary reminded him of his mother. So smitten was John that he prolonged the visit and missed his ship.

Months later he was impressed into the British navy. In 1745, midshipman Newton set sail for the East Indies on the H.M.S. *Harwich*. The voyage was to last five years, but a storm hit and the *Harwich* had to anchor off Plymouth, England. Newton was put in charge of a boat going ashore, with instructions to see that none of the crew deserted. Lovesick and headstrong, John himself escaped. Afraid to ask for directions to Chatham, he walked for two days before he was arrested by a military patrol and returned to the *Harwich*. There he was put into irons, stripped and flogged as a deserter, then transferred to a ship that ranked lowest in the maritime world—a ship engaged in the slave trade. "From this time I was exceedingly vile," he later confessed.

The female slaves on board were at the crew's disposal. John Newton, not quite 20 and now a militant atheist, indulged his sexual appetites as often as he wished. He was a far cry from the studious child who had sung hymns at his mother's knee.

In Sierra Leone, he left the ship to work for a slave dealer, a white man named Clow. Clow's common-law African wife hated John; when he fell desperately ill, she denied him food and water, and had her own black slaves torment him. Miraculously, Newton survived, but only to live in virtual bondage for more than a year on Clow's plantation. His life had reached its nadir.

Newton's father had urged a ship-owning friend in Liverpool to ask all captains of his slave ships working along the African coast to search for John and to bring him home. In February 1747 the ship *Greyhound* put in at a port in Sierra Leone, and Newton—through a series of divine interventions, he would later say—was found.

The *Greyhound* was on a long trade cruise, returning to England via Brazil. Seeking something to do, Newton began reading *The Imitation of Christ*, by Thomas à Kempis, a classic study of spiritual life that included warnings of God's judgment. Disturbed by the book's message, he flung it aside. It was March 9, 1748, the turning point of Newton's life.

In the dark, early-morning hours of the next day, the *Greyhound* was struck by a sea so heavy that part of her side was stove-in. "Pumping's useless! Nothing can save this ship, or us!" a veteran sailor exclaimed. But Newton and others did pump from 5 a.m. until noon. "If this will not do, the Lord have mercy upon us!" Newton cried out, startled by his own words.

The *Greyhound* did survive, and when she finally limped into Liverpool she carried a different John Newton from "the blasphemer" who had been plucked from the African coast. As he later explained, "I began to know there is a God that hears and answers prayer ... though I can see no reason why the Lord singled me out for mercy." (For the rest of Newton's life, he prayed and fasted on each anniversary of that fateful March morning.)

Newton rushed to Chatham to see Mary, and after a voyage as first mate on a slave ship, John Newton, 24, married Mary Catlett, 20.

For the next four years, John captained slave ships. At first he had no scruples about slave trading, which was considered respectable and essential to Britain's prosperity. But as his new faith steadily grew, he wrestled with his conscience. Twice each Sunday he began conducting his white crew in prayers as the chained Africans lay closely packed, some of them dying, on the opposite side of the ship.

During his next two voyages to Guinea, buying and selling blacks, he tried to act mercifully toward them. Then in 1754, while Newton was sitting at home drinking tea with Mary, he suffered a minor stroke. He recovered, but it was clear that his days at sea were over.

Newton was appointed the official Liverpool tide surveyor in 1755. With time on his hands, he studied Latin, mathematics and the Scriptures. He also wrote hymns and began to preach occasionally as a lay evangelist. Increasingly he felt the call to enter the ministry.

In 1764 the new Rev. John Newton, 39, was appointed the curate of Olney, a little village on the bank of the River Ouse in Buckinghamshire. Newton loved his Olney parishioners. "Brothers and sisters" he called them. Many were poor, uneducated lacemakers. Not only did he wear his old sea coat on his rounds to the sick and needy, but he also told stories from the pulpit of his seafaring life, his great sins and his own unworthiness to preach the Gospel.

Moreover, Newton dared to replace the conventional psalm-singing with the singing of hymns that were simple enough to be

Model of the slave ship *Brookes* that William Wilberforce used to demonstrate to the House of Commons the inhumane conditions captives endured on the Middle Passage.

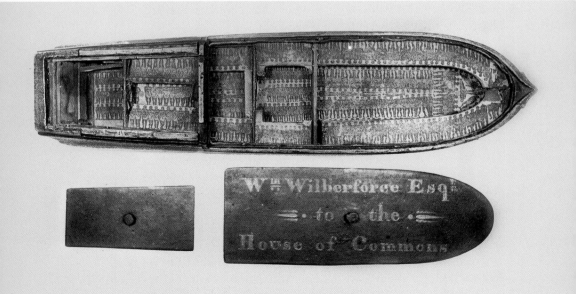

understood and felt by the plain people. When Newton published *An Authentic Narrative* in 1764, a graphic first-person record of his past debauchery and rescue, so many people flocked to his church that a new gallery had to be added.

After 15 years, Newton of Olney was reassigned to St. Mary Woolnoth, a distinguished church in London. Though his new position brought him great influence and social status, he never lost the image of himself broken and wretched on the coast of Africa, hating God and his own soul. His constant message, even to London's elite, was that he himself was living proof God could save the very worst.

In 1785, in yet another twist of fate, Newton crossed paths with a popular young political figure named William Wilberforce. Only 26 and already a member of Parliament, Wilberforce had recently experienced a religious awakening. Though his friends predicted a great political career, Wilberforce was convinced that his privileged life had no purpose.

Years before, Newton had been a friend and neighbor of Wilberforce's aunt, and as a youngster William had come under Newton's spell. Now "reborn," Wilberforce sought out the 60-year-old Newton for spiritual counsel. Should he resign from Parliament and enter the ministry? No, advised Newton. God can make you "a blessing both as a Christian and a statesman."

Wilberforce, who was looking for a cause, found it in Newton's sermons against slavery. This was an issue that no political party would dare touch, but no true Christian could evade.

Newton joined the battle as he could, though his health was failing. He alone in the political arena spoke from personal experience, a trump card the opposing forces were unable to counter. He addressed the Privy Council (including Prime Minister William Pitt): "The slaves lie in two rows, one above the other, on each side of the ship, like books upon a shelf. The poor creatures are in irons, both hands and feet. ... And every morning more instances than one are found of the living and the dead fastened together."

In March 1807, Parliament passed Wilberforce's bill abolishing the slave trade on British ships. That same year, on December 21, the Rev. John Newton, 82, spoke his last words: "I am a great sinner ... and Christ is a great Saviour."

Newton was buried beneath his church of St. Mary Woolnoth,

> Newton's first-person account of his debauchery and rescue drew so many people to his church, a new gallery was added.

and a tablet was placed on the church wall, with an inscription he had written himself: "John Newton, clerk, once an infidel and libertine, a servant of slaves in Africa, was by the rich mercy of our Lord and Saviour Jesus Christ preserved, restored, pardoned, and appointed to preach the faith he had long labored to destroy."

My research brought me to St. Mary Woolnoth. I stood on the very rostrum where the Rev. John Newton had held his congregation spellbound with stories of the sea, his sins and God's great mercy. As I looked out over the empty pews, the organist played the melodies of Newton's hymns. One glorious tune swelled up all around me. The verses were written at Olney—a minor autobiographical lyric that critics say is a poor example of Newton's work. But that hymn has traveled the world, bringing a message of hope and forgiveness to all people of faith.

I sang to myself the simple words I had learned as a child in a black church in the American South. You know them too:

> *Amazing grace—how sweet the*
> *sound—*
> *That saved a wretch like me!*
> *I once was lost, but now am*
> *found,*
> *Was blind, but now I see.* ✦

The Shadowland of Dreams

Long ago, when I was down on my luck, I learned what it takes to stay the course

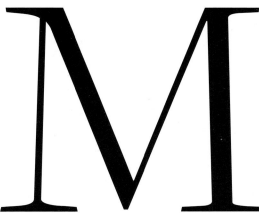

Many a young person tells me he wants to be a writer. I always encourage such people, but I also explain that there's a big difference between "being a writer" and writing. In most cases these individuals are dreaming of wealth and fame, not the long hours alone at a typewriter. "You've got to want to *write*," I say to them, "not want to be a *writer*."

The reality is that writing is a lonely, private and poor-paying affair. For every writer kissed by fortune there are thousands more whose longing is never requited. Even those who succeed often know long periods of neglect and poverty. I did.

When I left a 20-year career in the Coast Guard to become a

Published in Reader's Digest, August 1991

I reached into my cupboard— an orange crate nailed to the wall—and pulled out two cans of sardines. That and 18 cents was all that I had.

freelance writer, I had no prospects at all. What I did have was a friend in New York City, George Sims, with whom I'd grown up in Henning, Tennessee. George found me my home, a cleaned-out storage room in the Greenwich Village apartment building where he worked as superintendent. It didn't even matter that it was cold and had no bathroom. I immediately bought a used manual typewriter and felt like a genuine writer.

After a year or so, however, I still hadn't gotten a break and began to doubt myself. It was so hard to sell a story that I barely made enough to eat. But I knew I wanted to write. I had dreamed about it for years. I wasn't going to be one of those people who die wondering, *What if?* I would keep putting my dream to the test— even though it meant living with uncertainty and fear of failure. This is the Shadowland of hope, and anyone with a dream must learn to live there.

Then one day I got a call that changed my life. It wasn't an agent or editor offering a big contract. It was the opposite—a kind of siren call tempting me to give up my dream. On the phone was an old acquaintance from the Coast Guard, now stationed in San Francisco. He had once lent me a few bucks and liked to egg me about it. "When am I going to get that $15, Alex?" he teased.

"Next time I make a sale."

"I have a better idea," he said. "We need a new public information assistant out here, and we're paying $6000 a year. If you want it, you can have it."

Six thousand a year! That was real money in 1960. I could get a nice apartment, a used car, pay off debts and maybe save a little something. What's more, I could write on the side.

As the dollars were dancing in my head, something cleared my senses. From deep inside a bull-headed resolution welled up. I had dreamed of being a writer—full time. And that's what I was going to be. "Thanks, but no," I heard myself saying. "I'm going to stick it out and write."

Afterward, as I paced around my little room, I started to feel like a fool. Reaching into my cupboard—an orange crate nailed to the wall—I pulled out all that was there: two cans of sardines. Plunging my hands in my pockets, I came up with 18 cents. I took the cans and coins and jammed them into a crumpled paper bag. *There, Alex,*

I said to myself. *There's everything you've made of yourself so far.* I'm not sure I've ever felt so low.

I wish I could say things started getting better right away. But they didn't. Thank goodness I had George to help me over the rough spots.

Through him I met other struggling artists like Joe Delaney, a veteran painter from Knoxville, Tennessee. Often Joe lacked food money, so he'd visit a neighborhood butcher who would give him big bones with morsels of meat and a grocer who would hand him some wilted vegetables. That's all Joe needed to make down-home soup.

Another Village neighbor was a handsome young singer who ran a struggling restaurant. Rumor had it that if a customer ordered steak the singer would dash to a supermarket across the street to buy one. His name was Harry Belafonte.

People like Delaney and Belafonte became role models for me. I learned that you had to make sacrifices and live creatively to keep working at your dream. That's what living in the Shadowland is all about.

As I absorbed the lesson, I gradually began to sell my articles. I was writing about what many people were talking about then: civil rights, black Americans and Africa. Soon, like birds flying south, my thoughts were drawn back to my childhood. In the silence of my room, I heard the voices of Grandma, Cousin Georgia, Aunt Plus, Aunt Liz, and Aunt Till as they told stories about our family and slavery.

These were stories that black Americans had tended to avoid before, and so I mostly kept them to myself. But one day at lunch with editors of *Reader's Digest* I told these stories of my grandmother and aunts and cousins; and I said that I had a dream to trace my family's history to the first African brought to these shores in chains. I left that lunch with a contract that would help support my research and writing for nine years.

It was a long, slow climb out of the shadows. Yet in 1976, 17 years after I left the Coast Guard, *Roots* was published. Instantly I had the kind of fame and success that few writers ever experience. The shadows had turned into dazzling limelight.

For the first time I had money and open doors everywhere. The phone rang all the time with new friends and new deals. I packed up and moved to Los Angeles, where I could help in the making of the *Roots* TV miniseries. It was a confusing, exhilarating time, and in a sense I was blinded by the light of my success.

Then one day, while unpacking, I came across a box filled with things I had owned years before in the Village. Inside was a brown paper bag.

I opened it, and there were two corroded sardine cans, a nickel, a dime and three pennies. Suddenly the past came flooding in like a riptide. I could picture myself once again huddled over the typewriter in that cold, bleak, one-room apartment. And I said to myself, *The things in this bag are part of my roots too. I can't ever forget that.*

I sent them out to be framed in Lucite. I keep that clear plastic case where I can see it every day. I can see it now above my office desk in Knoxville, along with the Pulitzer Prize; a portrait of nine Emmys awarded the TV production of *Roots*; and the Spingarn medal—the NAACP's highest honor. I'd be hard pressed to say which means the most to me. But only one reminds me of the courage and persistence it takes to stay the course in the Shadowland.

It's a lesson anyone with a dream should learn. ◆

Aboard the
African
Star

After working on the book for more than a decade, Haley was stuck—and desperate

I just love to get out in the ocean. You are really out there, thinking in ways you haven't thought before. The best writing I ever possibly could do was after *The Digest* helped me go to Africa and Europe, and I was not known and I could just take my time and nobody was pressing me. God, I don't know how long it took me. I was working slowly, slowly. When I had done all the research, nine years,

Edited from a talk at Reader's Digest, October 10, 1991, four months before Alex Haley's death

working in between doing articles for other magazines, I was ready to write. I didn't know where to go, didn't know what to do. I knew I had a monumental task. And I got on a cargo ship. I went from Long Beach, California, completely around South America and back to Long Beach. It was 91 days.

There's something about a ship. Usually I go out on freight ships, cargo ships. (I wouldn't get caught on a liner. How can you write with 800 people dancing?) But the freight ships carry a maximum of 12 people, and they tend to be very quiet people.

I work my principal hours from about 10:30 at night until daybreak. The world is yours at that point. Most all the passengers are asleep.

I had written from the birth of Kunta Kinte through his capture. And I had got into the habit of talking to the character. I knew Kunta. I knew everything about Kunta. I knew what he was going to do. What he had done. Everything. And so I would talk to him. And I had become so attached to him that I knew now I had to put him in the slave ship and bring him across the ocean. That was the next part of the book. And I just really couldn't quite bring myself to write that.

I was in San Francisco. I wrote about 40 pages and chunked it out. When you write well, it isn't a question so much of what you want to say, it's a question of feel. Does it feel like you want it to feel? The feel starts coming in somewhere around about the fourth rewrite.

I wrote, twice more, about 40 pages and threw it out. And I realized what my bother was: I couldn't bring myself to feel I was up to writing about Kunta Kinte in that slave ship and me in a high-rise apartment. I had to get closer to Kunta. I had run out of my money at *The Digest*, lying so many times about when I'd finish so I couldn't ask for any more. I don't know where I got the money from. I went to Africa. Put out the word I wanted to get a ship coming from Africa to Florida. I just wanted to simulate the crossing.

I went down to Liberia, and I got on a freight ship called ap-

propriately enough the *African Star*. She was carrying a partial cargo of raw rubber in bales. And I got on as a passenger. I couldn't tell the captain or the mate what I wanted to do because they couldn't allow me to do it.

But I found one hold that was just about a third full of cargo and there was an entryway into it with a metal ladder down to the bottom of the hold. Down in there they had a long, wide, thick piece of rough sawed timber. They called it *dunnage*. It's used between cargo to keep it from shifting in rough seas.

After dinner the first night, I made my way down to this hold. I had a little pocket light. I took off my clothing to my underwear and lay down on my back on this piece of dunnage. I imagined I'm Kunta Kinte. I lay there and I got cold and colder. Nothing seemed to come except how ridiculous it was that I was doing this. By morning I had a terrible cold. I went back up. And the next night I'm down there doing the same thing.

While on a freighter, lying in the hold, Haley was able to simulate Kunta Kinte's slave-ship experience.

ALEX HALEY / ABOARD THE *AFRICAN STAR*

And then a startling thought came to me: All I had to do was step through the rail and drop in the sea.

Well, the third night when I left the dinner table, I couldn't make myself go back down in that hold. I just felt so miserable. I don't think I ever felt quite so bad. And instead of going down in the hold, I went to the stern of the ship. And I'm standing up there with my hands on the rail and looking down where the propellers are beating up this white froth. And in the froth are little luminous green phosphorescences. At sea you see that a lot. And I'm standing there looking at it, and all of a sudden it looked like all my troubles just came on me. I owed everybody I knew. Everybody was on my case. Why don't you finish this foolish thing? You ought not be doing it in the first place, writing about black genealogy. That's crazy.

I was just utterly miserable. Didn't feel like I had a friend in the world. And then a thought came to me that was startling. It wasn't frightening. It was just startling. I thought to myself, Hey, there's a cure for all this. You don't have to go through all this mess. All I had to do was step through the rail and drop in the sea.

Once having thought it, I began to feel quite good about it. I guess I was half a second before dropping in the sea. Fine, that would take care of it. You won't owe anybody anything. To hell with the publishers and the editors.

And I began to hear voices. They were not strident. They were just conversational. And I somehow knew every one of them. And they were saying things like, No, don't do that. No, you're doing the best you can. You just keep going.

And I knew exactly who they were. They were Grandma, Chicken George, Kunta Kinte. They were my cousin, Georgia, who lived in Kansas City and had passed away. They were all these people whom I had been writing about. They were talking to me. It was like in a dream.

I remember fighting myself loose from that rail, turning around, and I went scuttling like a crab up over the hatch. And finally I made my way back to my little stateroom and pitched down, head first, face first, belly first on the bunk, and I cried dry. I cried more I guess than I've cried since I was four years old.

And it was about midnight when I kind of got myself together. Then I got up, and the feeling was you have been assessed and you have been tried and you've been approved by all them who went before. So go ahead. And then I went back down in the hold. I had a terrible head cold, flu-ish like. I had with me a long yellow tablet and some pencils. This time I did not take my clothing off like I'd been doing. I kept them on because I was having such a bad cold. I lay down on the piece of timber.

Now Kunta Kinte was lying in this position on a shelf in the ship, the *Lord Ligonier*. She had left the Gambia River, July 5, 1767. She sailed two months, three weeks, two days. Destination Annapolis, Maryland. And he was lying there. And others were in there with him whom he knew. And what would he think?

What would be some of the things they would say? And when they would come to me in the dark, I would write. And that was how I did every night, only ten nights. From there to Florida. I remember rushing through the big, big Miami Airport. Flew back to San Francisco. Got with a doctor, and he kind of patched me up.

I sat down with those long yellow tablets and transcribed. And I began to write the chapter in *Roots* where Kunta Kinte crossed the ocean in a slave ship. That was probably the most emotional experience I had in the whole thing.

Come around about 1:30 in the morning, you've been working since 10:30 and decide you're going to take a little break. So you get up and you walk up on the deck. And you put your hand on the top rail, your foot on the bottom rail, and you look up. The first most striking thing is, man, you look up and there are heavenly objects as you never saw them before. You find yourself looking at planets at sea. And what you start to realize, you never saw clear air before. In some latitudes, down off West Africa, South America, on the night of a full moon, there are times when you get into an illusion—if you could just stretch a little further you feel like you could touch it. And you are out there amidst all God's firmament and then you stand and you feel through the sole of your shoe a fine vibration and you realize that's man at work. That's a huge diesel turbine, 35 feet down under the water driving this ship like a small island through the water. Still standing there, now you start hearing a slight hissing sound. You realize that's the skin of the ship cutting through the resistance of the ocean. With all that going on, feeling these man things and seeing the God things, that's about as close to holy as you are going to ever get. ✦

My Search for Roots

The earliest memory I have is Grandma, Cousin Georgia, Aunt Plus, Aunt Liz and Aunt Till talking on our front porch in Henning, Tenn. At dusk, these wrinkled, graying old ladies would sit in rocking chairs and talk, about slaves and massas and plantations—pieces and patches of family history, passed down across the generations by word of mouth. "Old-timey stuff," Mama would exclaim. She wanted no part of it.

The furthest-back person Grandma and the others ever mentioned was "the African." They would tell how he was brought here on a ship to a place called "Naplis" and sold as a slave in Virginia. There he mated with another slave, and had a little girl named Kizzy.

When Kizzy became four or five, the old ladies said, her father would point out to her various objects and name them in his native tongue. For example, he would point to a guitar and make

WILL CROCKETT

Published in Reader's Digest, May 1974

a single-syllable sound, *ko*. Pointing to a river that ran near the plantation, he'd say "Kamby Bolongo." And when other slaves addressed him as Toby—the name given him by his massa—the African would strenuously reject it, insisting that his name was "Kin-tay."

Kin-tay often told Kizzy stories about himself. He said that he had been near his village in Africa, chopping wood to make a drum, when he had been set upon by four men, overwhelmed, and kid-

A pensive Haley inside the Slave House on Goree Island, Senegal. Captured Africans passed through this holding and transfer point before they were shipped to the New World.

napped into slavery. When Kizzy grew up and became a mother, she told her son these stories, and he in turn would tell *his* children. His granddaughter became my grandmother, and she pumped that saga into me as if it were plasma, until I knew by rote the story of the African, and the subsequent generational wending of our family through cotton and tobacco plantations into the Civil War and then freedom.

At 17, during World War II, I enlisted in the Coast Guard, and found myself a messboy on a ship in the Southwest Pacific. To fight boredom, I began to teach myself to become a writer. I stayed on in the service after the war, writing every single night, seven nights a week, for eight years before I sold a story to a magazine. My first story in *The Digest* was published in June 1954: "The Harlem Nobody Knows." At age 37, I retired from military service, determined to be a full-time writer. Working with the famous Black

Muslim spokesman, I did the actual writing for the book *The Autobiography of Malcolm X*.

I remembered still the vivid highlights of my family's story. Could this account possibly be documented for a book? During 1962, between other assignments, I began following the story's trail. In plantation records, wills, census records, I documented bits here, shreds there. By now, Grandma was dead; repeatedly I visited other close sources, most notably our encyclopedic matriarch, "Cousin Georgia" Anderson in Kansas City, Kansas. I went as often as I could to the National Archives in Washington, and the Library of Congress, and the Daughters of the American Revolution Library.

By 1967, I felt I had the seven generations of the U.S. side documented. But the unknown quotient in the riddle of the past continued to be those strange, sharp, angular sounds spoken by the African himself. Since I lived in New York City, I began going to the United Nations lobby, stopping Africans and asking if they recognized the sounds. Every one of them listened to me, then quickly took off. I can well understand: me with a Tennessee accent, trying to imitate African sounds!

Finally, I sought out a linguistics expert who specialized in African languages. To him I repeated the phrases. The sound "Kin-tay," he said, was a Mandinka tribe surname. And "Kamby Bolongo" was probably the Gambia River in Mandinka dialect. Three days later, I was in Africa.

In Banjul, the capital of Gambia, I met with a group of Gambians. They told me how for centuries the history of Africa has been preserved. In the older villages of the back country there are old men, called *griots*, who are in effect living archives. Such men know and, on special occasions, tell the cumulative histories of clans, or families, or villages, as those histories have long been told. Since my forefather had said his name was Kin-tay (properly spelled Kinte), and since the Kinte clan was known in Gambia, they would see what they could do to help me.

I was back in New York when a registered letter came from Gambia. Word had been passed in the back country, and a *griot* of the Kinte clan had, indeed, been found. His name, the letter said, was Kebba Kanga Fofana. I returned to Gambia and organized a safari to locate him.

> Kin-tay often said he had been near his village, chopping wood to make a drum, when four men kidnapped him into slavery.

In Gambia, Alex Haley carries a Kinte child while flanked by his brothers, Julius, on his left, and George, on his right.

There is an expression called "the peak experience," a moment which, emotionally, can never again be equaled in your life. I had mine, that first day in the village of Juffure, in the back country in black West Africa.

When our 14-man safari arrived within sight of the village, the people came flocking out of their circular mud huts. From a distance I could see a small, old man with a pillbox hat, an off-white robe and an aura of "somebodiness" about him. The people quickly gathered around me in a kind of horseshoe pattern. The old man looked piercingly into my eyes, and he spoke in Mandinka. Translation came from the interpreters I had brought with me.

"Yes, we have been told by the forefathers that there are many of us from this place who are in exile in that place called America."

Then the old man, who was 73 rains of age—the Gambian way of saying 73 years old, based upon the one rainy season per year—began to tell me the lengthy ancestral history of the Kinte clan. It was clearly a formal occasion for the villagers. They had grown mouse-quiet, and stood rigidly.

Out of the *griot's* head came spilling lineage details incredible to hear. He recited who married whom, two or even three centuries back. I was struck not only by the profusion of details, but also by the Biblical pattern of the way he was speaking. It was something like, "—and so-and-so took as a wife so-and-so, and begat so-and-so. ..."

The *griot* had talked for some hours, and had got to about 1750 in our calendar. Now he said, through an interpreter, "About the time the king's soldiers came, the eldest of Omoro's four sons, Kunta, went away from this village to chop wood—and he was never seen again. ..."

Goose pimples came out on me the size of marbles. He just had no way in the world of knowing that what he told me meshed with what I'd heard from the old ladies on the front porch in Henning, Tennessee. I got out my notebook, which had in it what Grandma had said about the African. One of the interpreters showed it to the others, and they went to the *griot*, and they all got agitated. Then the *griot* went to the people, and they all got agitated.

I don't remember anyone giving an order, but those 70-odd people formed a ring around me, moving counterclockwise, chanting, their bodies close together. I can't begin to describe how I felt. A woman broke from the circle, a scowl on her jet-black face, and came charging toward me. She took her baby and almost roughly thrust it out at me. The gesture meant "Take it!" and I did, clasping the baby to me. Whereupon the woman all but snatched the baby away. Another woman did the same with her baby, then another, and another.

A year later, a famous professor at Harvard would tell me: "You were participating in one of the oldest ceremonies of humankind,

ALEX HALEY / MY SEARCH FOR ROOTS

A Return of the Shipping arrived at and

Nº	when arrived	Ships Names	Masters Names	Bur. then	where belongs	where
17		Brig James	Capt. Vongster	140	Bristol	Ganim
18	Sept. 10	Lord Ligonier	Capt. Davies	170	Gambia	London
19	Oct. 28	Montego Bay	Capt. Trenham	400	London	Senga

called 'the laying on of hands.' In their way, these tribespeople were saying to you, 'Through this flesh, which is us, we are you and you are us.'"

Later, as we drove out over the back-country road, I heard the staccato sound of drums. When we approached the next village, people were packed alongside the dusty road, waving, and the din from them welled louder as we came closer. As I stood up in the Land Rover, I finally realized what it was they were all shouting: "Meester Kinte! Meester Kinte!" In their eyes I was the symbol of all black people in the United States whose forefathers had been torn out of Africa while theirs remained.

Hands before my face, I began crying—crying as I have never cried in my life. Right at that time, crying was all I could do.

I went then to London. I searched and searched, and finally in the British Parliamentary records, I found that the "king's soldiers" mentioned by the *griot* referred to a group called "Colonel O'Hare's forces," which had been sent up the Gambia River in 1767 to guard the then British-operated James Fort, a slave fort.

I next went to Lloyds of London, where doors were opened for me to research among all kinds of old maritime records. I pored through the records of slave ships that had sailed from Africa. Volumes upon volumes of these records exist. One afternoon about 2:30, during the seventh week of searching, I was going through my 1023rd set of ship records. I picked up a sheet that had on it the reported movements of 30 slave ships, my eyes stopped at No. 18, and my glance swept across the column entries. This vessel had sailed directly from the Gambia River to

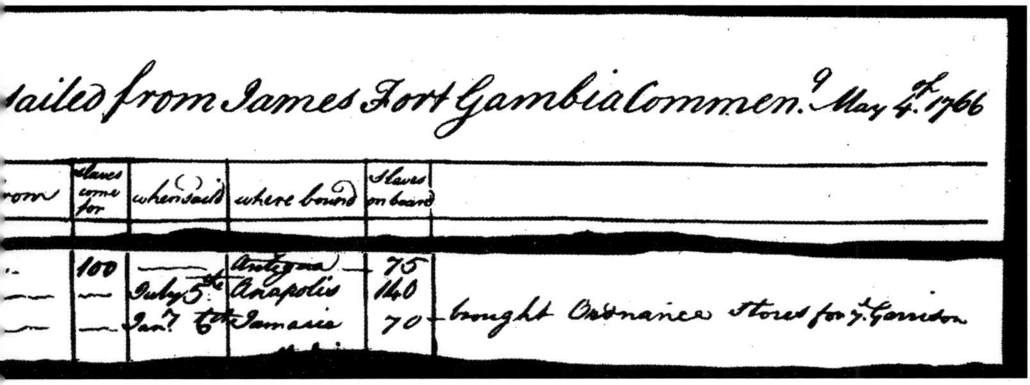

Caption from table (handwritten): Sailed from James Fort Gambia Commen. 9 May 4th 1766

from	Slaves come for	when said	where bound	Slaves on board	
	100	July 5th	Antigua / Anapolis	75 / 140	
		Jan 6th	Jamaica	70	brought Ordnance Stores for ye Garrison.

America in 1767; her name was the *Lord Ligonier*; and she had arrived at Annapolis (Naplis) the morning of September 29, 1767.

Exactly 200 years later, on September 29, 1967, there was nowhere in the world for me to be except standing on a pier at Annapolis, staring seaward across those waters over which my great-great-great-great-grandfather had been brought. And there in Annapolis I inspected the microfilmed records of the Maryland *Gazette*. In the issue of October 1, 1767, on page 3, I found an advertisement informing readers that the *Lord Ligonier* had just arrived from the River Gambia, with "a cargo of choice, healthy slaves" to be sold at auction the following Wednesday.

In the years since, I have done extensive research in 50 or so libraries, archives and repositories on three continents. I spent a year combing through countless documents to learn about the culture of Gambia's villages in the 18th and 19th centuries. Desiring to sail over the same waters navigated by the *Lord Ligonier*, I flew to Africa and boarded the freighter *African Star*. I forced myself to spend the ten nights of the crossing in the cold, dark cargo hold, stripped to my underwear, lying on my back on a rough, bare plank. But this was sheer luxury compared to the inhuman ordeal suffered by those millions who, chained and shackled, lay in terror and in their own filth in the stinking darkness through voyages averaging 60 to 70 days.

This book has taken me ten years and more. Why have I called it *Roots*? Because it not only tells the story of a family, my own, but also symbolizes the history of millions of American blacks of African descent. I intend my book to be a buoy for black self-esteem—and a reminder of the universal truth that we are all descendants of the same Creator. ◆

This page, from an old registry, records ship traffic at James Fort, Gambia, a slave port. No. 18, *Lord Ligonier*, arrived September 13, 1766, and sailed for Annapolis, Maryland, on July 5, 1767.

The
Legacy

Haley's Pulitzer Prize-winning book and the Emmy Award-winning TV miniseries helped to define the post-civil rights era discussion of race more than any other work of that decade. *Roots* made the history of black-white relations accessible and understandable to people of all ethnic backgrounds and all ages. In this section, Haley also writes about what this great work meant to him. And the editors of *Reader's Digest* asked a number of notable people, in politics, entertainment, medicine, sports and business, to comment on how the book changed their lives.

Fort James, on
James Island,
Gambia. The fort
was used as a
trading base for
gold and ivory,
then slaves.

Roots

FROM THE BOOK

An American family's story
of survival and triumph

Published in Reader's Digest, May and June 1974, April and May 1977

Early in the spring of 1750, in the village of Juffure, four days upriver from the coast of Gambia, West Africa, a man-child was born to Omoro Kinte and Binta Kebba. Forcing forth from Binta's strong young body, he was as black as she was, flecked and slippery with her blood, and he was bawling. The two wrinkled mid-wives, old Nyo Boto and the baby's paternal grandmother, Yaisa, saw that it was a boy and cackled with joy. According to the forefathers, who had followed Muhammad's teachings through hundreds of an-nual rains, a boy firstborn presaged the special blessings of Allah.

It was the hour before the first crowing of the cocks. The thin blue smoke of cooking fires went curling up, pungent and pleasant, over the small dusty village of round mud huts. The men filed briskly to the praying place where the *alimamo*, the village's holy man, led the first of the five daily Muslim prayers: *"Allahu akbar! Ashadu an lawilahala!"* ("Allah is great! I bear witness that there is only one Allah!") And afterward Omoro rushed among them, beaming and excited, to tell them of his firstborn son.

By ancient custom, for the next seven days Omoro occupied himself with selecting a name for his son. It would have to be a name rich with history and promise, for the people of his tribe—the Mandinkas—believed that a child would develop seven of the characteristics of his namesake.

When the eighth day arrived, the villagers gathered in the early evening before Omoro's hut. As Binta proudly held her infant, a small patch of his first hair was shaved off, as was always done, and the women exclaimed at how well-formed the baby was. Then the village drummer began to beat his small *tan-tang* drums.

The *alimamo* said a prayer over the calabashes of boiled grain and *munko* cakes of pounded rice and honey brought as gifts by the villagers. Next he prayed over the infant, entreating Allah to grant him long life and the strength and spirit to bring honor to the name he was about to receive.

Omoro then walked to his wife's side, leaned over the infant and, as all watched, whispered into his son's ear the name he had chosen for him. Omoro's people felt that each human being should be the first to know who he was.

The drum resounded again, and now Omoro whispered the name into Binta's ear, and Binta smiled with pride. Then he whispered the name to the village schoolmaster, who announced: "The first child of Omoro Kinte and Binta Kebba is named Kunta!"

It was the name of the child's late paternal grandfather, Kairaba Kunta Kinte, who had come from his native Mauretania into Gambia, where his unending prayers for five days had saved the people of Juffure from a famine. He had married Yaisa, and had served Juffure honorably as the *alimamo* until his death. All the people proclaimed their admiration and respect for such distinguished lineage.

That night, out under the moon and stars, Omoro completed the naming ritual. By the small mosque of mud and thatch, he lifted his baby to the heavens and said: "Behold—the only thing greater than yourself."

In her hut each evening, Binta would soften her baby's skin by greasing him from head to toe with shea-tree butter, then carry him proudly across the village to the hut of Grandma Yaisa. The two of them would set little Kunta to whimpering with their repeated pinchings and pressings of his little head, nose, ears and lips to shape them correctly.

Sometimes Omoro would take his son away from the women to his own hut—husbands always resided separately from their wives—where he let the child's eyes and fingers explore his huntsman's bag, covered with cowrie shells, and the dark, slender spear whose shaft was polished from much use. Omoro talked to Kunta of the fine and brave deeds he would perform when he grew up.

When he was 13 moons, Kunta tried his first unsteady steps. Before long, he was able to toddle about without an assisting hand. Three annual rains passed. Little Kunta spent his days romping under the watchful eyes of the old grandmothers who took care of what was called the first *kafo*, which included all the children under five rains in age. The boys and girls scampered about as naked as animals. Laughing and squealing, they played hide-and-seek and scattered the dogs and chickens, chasing them along the inside wall of the tall bamboo fence that enclosed the village.

But all the children would scramble to sit still and quiet when the telling of a story was promised by one of the grandmothers, especially the beloved Nyo Boto. Baldheaded, deeply wrinkled, as black as the bottom of an old cooking pot, her few remaining teeth a deep orange from the countless kola nuts she had gnawed on, Nyo Boto would settle herself with much grunting on her low stool and begin a story in the same way that all Mandinka storytellers began: "At this certain time, in this certain village, lived this certain person. ..."

It was old Nyo Boto who told of the terrible time she remembered when there was not enough rain. Although the people prayed hard to Allah and the women danced the ancestral rain dance and sacrificed two goats and a bullock every day, still everything growing began to parch. Even the forest water holes dried up, and wild animals appeared at the village well. More and more people grew ill, and the old and weak began to die.

It was then, said Nyo Boto, that Allah guided the steps of Kairaba Kunta Kinte to the village. Seeing the people's plight, he knelt down and prayed to Allah—almost without sleep, and taking only a few sips of water as nourishment—for the next five days. And on the evening of the fifth day came a great rain, which fell like a flood and saved Juffure.

When she had finished her story, the other children looked with new respect at Kunta, who bore that honored name.

"Tastier Than Goat!"

The seasons came and went. First, the planting season, when Binta and the other wives hurried to the dugout canoes on the banks of the village *bolong*, one of the many tributary canals that twisted inland from the Gambia River, and paddled to the fields where generations of Juffure women had grown their rice. In other fields the men had piled tall stacks of dry weeds and set them afire to nourish the soil; and now, as the first light rains began to fall, they put out their groundnuts and other seeds. And then the big rains came. And after that the harvest, and the long, scorching dry spell.

Kunta and his *kafo* mates began to feel older than their rains of age, which now ranged from five to nine. They envied the older boys of the third *kafo* their goatherding jobs and their *dundikos*—long cotton robes—and thought themselves too grown up to be made to go naked any longer. They avoided babies like Kunta's new brother Lamin as if they were diseased, and began hanging around adults in hopes of being sent off on an errand.

It was on the morning of the second day of the harvest, just as Kunta began to walk out the door of his mother's hut, that Binta said to him gruffly, "Why don't you put on your clothes?" Kunta turned around abruptly. There, hanging from a peg, he saw a brand-new *dundiko*. Struggling to conceal his excitement, he put it on and sauntered out the door. Others of his *kafo* were already outside—several, like him, dressed for the first time in their lives, leaping, shouting and laughing because their nakedness was covered at last. They were now officially of the second *kafo*. They were becoming men.

The next day, when Omoro handed Kunta a new slingshot, his breath all but choked off. He stood looking up in awe at his father, not knowing what to say, and Omoro spoke: "As you are now second *kafo*, it means you will go to school and tend goats. You go today with Toumani Touray."

Kunta dashed away and joined his *kafo* mates. They clustered about the goat pens where the older boys were opening the gates for the day's grazing. With the help of *wuolo* dogs, they soon had the blatting goats hurrying down the dusty path. Kunta's *kafo* ran uncertainly behind.

Toumani Touray acted as if Kunta were some kind of insect. "Do you know the value of a goat?" he asked, and before Kunta could admit he wasn't sure, "Well, if you lose one, your father will let you know." And Toumani Touray launched into a lecture on goatherding. If a goat was allowed to stray into the forest, he said, there were lions and panthers which with a single spring from the grass could tear a goat apart. "And if a boy is close enough, he is tastier than a goat!"

The next morning, Kunta and his mates began their religious education. The schoolmaster, Brima Cesay, told them, "You are no longer children, but are of the second *kafo*, meaning you have responsibilities." With that evening's class he would begin to read to them certain verses of the Koran, which they must memorize. Now, between the goats all day, the schoolmaster after breakfast and late in the afternoon, and what slingshot practice Kunta could manage before darkness, there was little time for play. With the annual seven-day harvest festival less than a moon away, Kunta was also forced to tend his pesky little brother Lamin for several evenings, while his mother spun cotton which the men would weave for new clothes for the family.

The morning after the new moon, the big ceremonial *tobalo* drum sounded at dawn. The harvest festival began with dancing, and Kunta's eyes widened as he saw his father join a throng of whirling, leaping bodies, some wearing horrifying costumes and masks, some not. Omoro's knees were churning high, his feet stomping up dust. With ripping cries he reared backward, muscles trembling, then lunged forward, hammering at his chest, and went leaping and twisting into the air, landing with heavy grunts.

Kunta had seen such ceremonies for many harvests, plantings, men leaving to hunt, and for weddings, births and deaths, but the dancing had never moved him as it did now. The beat of the *tan-tang* drums seemed to throb in his limbs. As if it were a dream, he felt his body begin to quiver and his arms to flail, and soon he was springing and shouting along with the others. From the very young to the very old, everyone danced on through the entire day.

> Kunta watched in terror as one man emerged from each hut pulling a trembling boy.

The festival continued for six more days with parades, feasting, wrestling, trading, and storytelling by traveling *griots* who sang endless verses of ancient kings and family clans, of great battles and legends of the past. Every day brought traveling musicians, experts on the 24-stringed *cora* and the *balafon*, a melodious instrument made of gourds that were struck with mallets.

On the final day, Kunta was awakened by the sound of screams. Pulling on his *dundiko*, he went dashing out. Before several of the huts were half a dozen men in fierce masks, tall headdresses and costumes of leaf and bark. Kunta watched in terror as one man entered each hut and emerged pulling a trembling boy of the third *kafo*, a heavy white cotton hood placed over his head. When all of the older boys had been collected, the men, yelling and shoving, carried them out through the village gate.

Kunta knew that every five years the older boys were taken away from Juffure for their manhood training, but he had no idea it was like this. In the days that followed, he and his *kafo* mates could think of nothing but the frightening things they had learned of the training.

They all had heard that many full moons would pass before the boys returned. It was also said that they got beatings daily, and that they were sent out alone at night into the deep forest. But the worst thing—a knowledge that made Kunta nervous every time he had to urinate—was that during manhood training a part of his *foto* would be cut off.

The Unknown Toubob

Two rains passed, and Binta's belly was big again. Her temper was shorter than usual, and Kunta was grateful each morning when goatherding and other tasks let him escape for a few hours. He couldn't help feeling sorry for Lamin, who was not old enough to go out of the house alone. So, one day he asked Binta if Lamin could join him on an errand.

After that, Kunta took his brother out nearly every day. He taught Lamin how to wrestle, how to whistle through his fingers, and showed him the kind of berry leaves from which his mother made tea. He cautioned him to take the big, shiny dung beetles they always saw crawling in the hut and set them gently on the ground, for it was very bad luck to harm them. To touch a rooster's spur was even worse luck.

Walking alongside, Lamin would ply Kunta with a steady stream of questions.

"Why does no one harm owls?"

"Because all our dead ancestors' spirits are in owls."

Now and then, Lamin asked something about which Kunta knew nothing at all: "Is the sun on fire?" Or, "Why doesn't our father sleep with us?" At such times, Kunta grunted and fell silent as Omoro did when he tired of Kunta's questions. But, later, he would ask his father for the answers.

"What are slaves?" Lamin asked one day. Kunta did not know. And so, the next day, he questioned his father. Omoro was silent for a long while. Finally, "Slaves are not always easy to tell from those who are not slaves," he replied. He told Kunta that people became slaves in different ways. Some were born of slave mothers—and he named several who lived in Juffure. Others, facing starvation in their own villages during the hungry season, had come to Juffure and begged to become the slaves of someone who would provide for them. Still others had been enemies and had been captured.

"Even so," Omoro said, "their rights are guaranteed by the laws of our forefathers," and he explained that all masters had to provide their slaves with food, clothing, a house, a farm plot to work on half-shares, and a wife or a husband. Also, slaves could buy their freedom with what they saved by farming. If they married into the family that owned them, they were assured that they would never be sold or given away.

But Kunta wanted to know more. Toumani Touray had told him about the hairy white men—the *toubob*—who sometimes burned villages and took people away. His father said nothing until, a few days later, he invited both Kunta and Lamin to go with him beyond the village to collect some roots.

Then he told them of a trip that he and his two brothers had taken many rains ago. They had trekked along the banks of the Gambia Bolongo, keeping carefully concealed.

At last they had come to a place where 20 great *toubob* canoes were moored in the river, each big enough to hold all the people of Juffure, each with a huge white cloth tied by ropes to a tree-like pole as tall as ten men. Many *toubob* were moving about, and *slatees*—black helpers—were with them. Small canoes were taking such things as dried indigo, cotton, beeswax and hides to the big canoes. More terrible than he could describe, however, said Omoro, were the beatings and other cruelties they saw being dealt out to those who had been captured for the *toubob* to take away.

Omoro looked at Kunta carefully. "Some Mandinkas sell their slaves to *toubob*," he said. "Such men are traitors. A Kinte must never do this."

Kunta and Lamin sat frozen with fear. "Papa," asked Lamin, "where do the big canoes take the stolen people?"

"The elders say to *toubabo doo*," said Omoro, "a land where slaves are sold to huge cannibals called *toubabo koomi*, who eat us. No man knows any more about it."

Journey of the New Moon

On a hot, quiet afternoon a few days later, there suddenly came a sharp burst of drums from the village. Kunta dashed to the hut of Juffure's drummer: Others had already gathered there to hear the news. A messenger from the next village was speaking to Omoro. Five days of walking the way the sun rose, Kunta's uncles Janneh and Saloum Kinte were building a new village; their brother Omoro was expected for the ceremonial blessing of the village on the second next new moon.

When the messenger had finished, Omoro gave his reply: Allah willing, he would be there.

Not many days before Omoro's departure, an idea almost too big to think about seized Kunta. Was it possible that Omoro might let *him* go, too? Now and then a boy was allowed to share a journey with his father, although never one so young as eight rains. Sensing that his mother would disapprove of his dream, Kunta knew that his only hope lay in asking his father directly.

As he tended his herd, three days before Omoro was to go, the almost despairing Kunta saw his father leave Binta's hut. Abandoning his goats, he ran like a hare and came to a breathless stop, looking up pleadingly at his father's startled face. Gulping, he couldn't remember a thing he had meant to say.

Omoro gazed at his son for a moment. Then, "I have just told your mother," he said—and walked on.

It took Kunta a few seconds to realize what his father meant. "Aiee!" he shouted. Dropping onto his belly, he sprang froglike into the air and bolted back to his goats. Then, suddenly, he grew quiet with the knowledge that ever since the message had come his father had been thinking about him.

On the morning of their departure, first Omoro, then Kunta, took two steps into the dust outside Omoro's hut. Turning and bending down, they scraped up the dust of their first footprints and put it into their hunters' bags, thus ensuring that their footprints would return to this place. Binta watched, weeping, from her doorway. As they walked through the village, Kunta started to turn for a last look. But, seeing that his father did not turn, he kept his eyes front and quickly strode along, nearly trotting to keep the proper two paces behind Omoro.

After about an hour, Kunta's excitement had waned almost as much as his pace. His head-bundle began to feel heavier and heavier, the muscles below his knees ached, and his face was sweating. When the sun had covered nearly half the sky, Kunta began to think he wasn't going to be able to keep up. A feeling of panic was rising in him when Omoro, who had neither spoken nor looked back, suddenly stopped and swung his head-load to the ground alongside a clear pool. There they sipped the cool spring water and roasted and ate four plump pigeons that Omoro had shot with his bow. Then they set out on the trail once more.

The gnarled branches and graceful form of thorn trees have become one of the familiar images of sub-Saharan Africa.

"*Toubob* brings his canoes one day of walking from here," said Omoro when they had gone a good distance. "Tonight we must sleep in a village." Omoro walked on even faster, his fingers touching his sheath knife.

The orange ball of the sun was nearing the earth when Omoro and Kunta sighted a thin trail of smoke from a village up ahead. As they approached, they could tell that something was not right. No children came running out to meet them. As they passed by the village baobab tree, Kunta saw that it was partly burned. More than half of the mud huts appeared to be empty, and the people of the village—most of them lying in the doorways of their huts—were all old or sick.

Several wrinkled old men weakly received the travelers. Interrupting each other in their haste, they began to explain what had happened. Slave traders had taken or killed all of their younger people. "From your rains to his!" one old man said, pointing at Omoro, then at Kunta. "We old ones they spared."

For the next three days, Omoro and Kunta walked steadily on, bypassing villages, sleeping near the trail on beds of soft branches.

It seemed to Kunta as if he had barely laid his head down before his father was shaking him awake in the early dawn. Kunta's feet were blistered now, and his whole body ached, but he pushed on behind Omoro, pretending that his manhood training had already begun, determined that he would be the last boy in his *kafo* to betray his pain.

On the fourth day, they came to a village where there was no one at all to be seen, and not a sound to be heard except for the birds and monkeys. Kunta waited in vain for Omoro to explain the mystery. It was the chattering children of the next village who finally did so. Pointing back down the trail, they said that the village's chief had kept on doing things his people disliked, until one night not long ago, as he slept, every family of that village quietly went away with all its possessions to the homes of friends and families in other places. They left behind an "empty chief," who was now going about begging his people to believe that, if they would only return, he would act better.

> His feet were blistered, his whole body ached, but he vowed he'd be the last boy in his *kafo* to betray his pain.

At this second village, Omoro arranged for the village drummer to send the announcement of their arrival to his brothers. They would understand that Omoro would soon be there, though they did not know that Kunta was with him. Kunta felt very proud that he had traveled so far with his father, and the sound of the drums telling of their visit would not leave his ears.

On the fifth day, just as the sun began to turn crimson at the western horizon, he spotted smoke rising from a village not far ahead. Soon he began to hear the distant thunder of a *tobalo* drum, the throb of smaller *tan-tang* drums and the loud clapping of dancers. Then the trail made a turn—and there was the village.

Kunta's feet scarcely felt the ground. The pounding of the drums grew louder and louder, and suddenly dancers appeared, grunting and shouting in their leaf-and-bark costumes, stamping out through the village gate to meet the distinguished visitors. Two figures came pushing through the crowd. Omoro's head-bundle dropped to the ground, and he hurried toward them. Before he knew it, Kunta dropped his own head-bundle and was running, too.

The two men and his father were hugging and pounding one another. "And who is this? Our brother's son?" Both men lifted Kunta off his feet and embraced him amid exclamations of joy. His uncle Saloum thumped his fist on Kunta's head. "Not since he got his name have we been together. And now look at him. How many rains have you, brother's son Kunta?"

"Eight rains, father's brother," Kunta answered politely.

"Nearly ready for manhood training!" exclaimed his uncle.

Soon it was dark, and the village fires were lighted, and the people gathered around them. Then Janneh and Saloum walked inside the circle of listeners and told stories of their adventures. Before building this village, they had been travelers and traders, for which the Mandinka were noted. They spoke of strange, humpbacked animals. "They are called camels," said Saloum, "and they live in a place of endless sand."

Janneh was unrolling a large piece of tanned hide on which was a drawing. "This is Africa," he said, and his finger traced what he told them was a great sand desert, a place many times larger than their kingdom.

To the north coast of Africa, the *toubob* ships brought porcelain, spices, cloth, horses and countless things made by machines, said Saloum. Then men, camels and donkeys bore those goods inland to places like Sijilmasa, Ghadames and Marrakesh. The moving finger of Janneh showed where those cities were.

Now Saloum took the tanned-hide drawing and began to trace locations with his finger as Janneh spoke. "Our own African goods are brought to many great cities—gold, ivory, skins, olives, dates, cotton, copper and precious stones. As we sit here tonight, there are many men with heavy head-loads crossing deep forests taking these things to the *toubob's* ships."

Looking as proud as his father beside him, Kunta listened with wonder, and then and there he vowed silently that someday he, too, would venture to such exciting places.

The White Hood

Kunta reached his 12th rain, and he and his *kafo* were about to complete the schooling they had received twice daily since they were five. When the day of graduation came, the parents of the boys seated themselves, beaming with pride, in the teacher's yard. Then Brima Cesay stood and looked around at his pupils. He asked Kunta a question.

"What was the profession of your ancient forefathers, Kunta Kinte?"

"Hundreds of rains ago in the land of Mali," Kunta confidently replied, "the Kinte men were blacksmiths, and their women were makers of pots and spinners of cotton."

Next there were riddles, and then the students wrote their names on slates in Arabic as they had been taught. Finally, the teacher asked each graduate to stand, calling out his name. "Kairaba Kunta Kinte." With all eyes upon him, Kunta felt the great pride of his family, in the front row of spectators, even of his ancestors in the burying ground beyond the village. He read aloud a verse from the Koran. Finishing, he pressed it to his forehead and said, "Amen." When the readings were done, everyone broke into wild cheering.

The passing moons flowed into seasons until yet another rain had passed, and Kunta's *kafo* had taught Lamin's *kafo* how to be goatherds. A time long awaited now drew steadily nearer, for the next harvest festival would end with the taking away of the third *kafo*—those boys between 10 and 15 rains in age. Kunta did his best to hide the vivid memory of that morning, five rains before, when he and his mates had been scared nearly out of their wits as they watched boys under white hoods being taken from the village by a band of masked, shrieking *kankurang* dancers.

The great *tobalo* drum soon sounded out the beginning of the new harvest, and Kunta joined the rest of the villagers in the fields. He welcomed the long days of hard work, for they kept him too busy and too tired to give much thought to what lay ahead. When the festival began, he found himself unable to enjoy the music and the dancing and the feasting as the others did.

On the night before the last day of the festival, Kunta was in Omoro's hut, finishing his evening meal, when his mother's brother walked in and stood behind him. From the corner of his eye, Kunta glimpsed his kinsman raising something white, and before he had a chance to turn around, a long hood had been pulled down over his head. The terror that shot through Kunta almost numbed him.

He felt a hand gripping his upper arm and urging him to stand up, then to move backward until he was pushed down onto a low stool.

He sat very still, trying to accustom himself to the darkness. It was quiet in the hut. He gulped down his fear, remembering that any boy who failed the manhood training would be treated as a child for the rest of his life, avoided, never permitted to marry lest he father others like himself.

Hours passed. The drumbeats and the shouting of the dancers in the distance ceased. He dozed, jerked awake with a start, and finally slipped into a fitful sleep.

When the *tobalo* boomed, he all but leaped from his skin. Now he could picture the morning's activities from the sounds his ears picked up—the crowing of the cocks, the barking of the *wuolo* dogs, the bumping of the women's pestles as they beat the breakfast grain. After a while, he heard the sound of people talking, louder and louder; then drums joined the din. A moment later, his heart seemed to stop as he sensed the sudden movement of someone rushing into the hut. His wrists were grabbed, and he was pushed out through the hut door into the deafening noise of drums and the blood-curdling whoops of the dancers. The noise receded, only to rise again to a frenzied pitch every time another boy was dragged from a hut.

Kunta's ears told him that he had joined a moving line of marchers, all stepping to the swift, sharp rhythm of the drums. As they passed through the village gates—he could tell because the noise of the crowd began to fade—he felt hot tears welling up and running down his cheeks. He knew that he was leaving behind more than his father and mother and his brothers and the village of his birth, and this filled him with sadness as much as terror.

But he knew it must be done, as it had been done by his father before him, and would someday be done by his son. He would return as a man—or not at all.

Between Fear and Anger

They must be approaching a bamboo grove, Kunta guessed. Through his hood he could smell the rich fragrance of freshly chopped stems. A few steps later, the pounding of the drums up ahead became muffled, as if they had entered an enclosure of some kind, and then the drums stopped and the marchers halted. For several minutes, everyone stood still and silent. Kunta remembered feeling like this once before, when his father, along the trail, had signaled for him to stand motionless until a pride of lions had passed them by in the dusk. He listened for the slightest sound that might tell him where they were, but all he could hear was the screeching of birds and the scolding of monkeys overhead.

Suddenly, Kunta's hood was lifted. He stood blinking in the bright sun of midafternoon. Directly before Kunta and his mates stood stern, wrinkled Silla Ba Dibba, one of the senior elders of Juffure. His eyes scanned their faces as he would have looked at crawling maggots. Kunta knew that this was surely their *kintango*, the man in charge of their manhood training. Widening his gaze for a moment—careful not to move his head—Kunta saw that they stood in a compound dotted with several thatch-roofed mud huts surrounded by a new bamboo fence.

"Children left Juffure village," said the *kintango* in a loud voice. "If men are to return, your fears must be erased, for a fearful person is a weak person, and a weak person is a danger to his tribe." He turned away, and as he did so, two of his helpers sprang forward and began to lay about among the boys with sticks, pummeling their shoulders and backsides as they herded the 23-boy *kafo* into the small mud huts.

Kunta and four other boys huddled in their hut for hours, not daring to speak. Just after sunset, as Kunta's belly was panging with hunger, the *kintango* helpers burst into the hut. "Move!" A stick caught him sharply across the shoulders as he rushed outside into the dusk. The *kintango* fixed them with a dark scowl and announced that they were about to undertake a night journey into the surrounding forest. At the order to march, the long line of boys set out along the path in clumsy disarray, and the sticks fell steadily among them.

It was almost dawn when the boys stumbled back into the *jujuo* compound. Every boy's feet bore big raw blisters. Kunta himself felt ready to die. He trudged to his hut, lost his footing, stumbled to the dirt floor—and fell asleep where he lay.

On the next few nights there were other marches, each longer than the last. The *kintango* showed them how men deep in the forest use the stars to guide them, and every boy of the *kafo* learned how to lead the group back to the *jujuo*.

Animals, the *kintango* told them, were the best teachers of the art of hunting. His helpers pointed out where lions had recently crouched in wait, showed the boys how to track antelope, and set

> "Children left Juffure village," the *kintango* said. "If men are to return, your fears must be erased."

the *kafo* to inspecting the cracks in rocks where wolves and hyenas hid. The boys were taught to imitate the sounds of animals and birds, and the air was rent with their grunts and whistles. Soon, every bite of meat they ate was either trapped by the boys or shot by their arrows.

But no matter how much they added to their knowledge and abilities, the old *kintango* was never satisfied. His demands and his discipline remained so strict that the boys were torn between fear and anger most of the time. Any command to one boy that was not instantly and perfectly performed brought a beating to the entire *kafo*. The only thing that kept Kunta and the others from giving that boy a beating of their own was the certain knowledge that they would be beaten for fighting. Among the first lessons they had learned in life—long before coming to the *jujuo*—was that Mandinkas must never fight among themselves.

Men of Juffure

It came without warning. One day, as the sun reached the noon-time position, one of the *kintango* helpers gave what seemed to be a routine order for the *kafo* to line up in the compound. The *kintango* came from his hut and walked before them.

"Hold out your *fotos*," he commanded. The time had come for that which Kunta dreaded: the *kasas boyo* operation which would purify a boy and prepare him to father many sons. They hesitated, not wanting to believe what they had heard. "Now!" he shouted. Slowly they obeyed, each keeping his eyes on the ground as he reached inside his loincloth.

Then the *kintango* helpers wrapped around the head of each boy's *foto* a short length of cloth spread with a green paste made of a pounded leaf. "Soon your *fotos* will have no feeling," the *kintango* said, ordering them back into their huts.

Huddled inside, ashamed and afraid, the boys waited in silence until about midafternoon, when again they were ordered outside, where they stood watching as a number of men from Juffure—fathers, older brothers and uncles—filed in through the gate, Omoro among them. The men formed a line facing the boys and chanted together: "This thing to be done…also has been done to us…as to the forefathers before us…so that you also will become…all of us men together." Then the *kintango* sent the boys back inside their huts.

ight was falling when they heard many drums suddenly begin to pound, and they were ordered outside again. The fathers, uncles and brothers stood nearby, this time chanting, "You soon will return home…and in time you will marry…and life everlasting will spring from your loins." The *kintango* assistant called out one boy's name and motioned him behind a long screen of woven bamboo. A few moments later, the boy reappeared—with a bloodstained cloth between his legs. Another boy's name was called, and another, and finally, "Kunta Kinte!"

He walked behind the screen. Here were four men, one of whom told him to lie down on his back. He did so—his shaking legs wouldn't have supported him any longer anyway. The men then leaned down, grasped him firmly, and lifted his thighs upward. Just before closing his eyes, Kunta saw the *kintango* bending over him with something in his hands. Then he felt the cutting pain. In a moment he was bandaged tightly, and his mother's brother helped him back outside. The thing he had feared above all else had now been done.

As the *fotos* of the *kafo* healed, a general air of jubilation rose within the *jujuo*; gone forever was the indignity of being mere boys in body as well as in mind. Now they were very nearly men. Even the *kintango* would say, "You men…" To Kunta and his mates, this was beautiful to hear.

"When your training is finished," said the *kintango* one evening, "you will begin to serve Juffure as its eyes and ears. You will be expected to stand guard over the village—beyond the gates—as lookouts for raiders and savages. You will also be responsible for inspecting the women's cooking pots to make sure they are kept clean, and you will be expected to reprimand them most severely if any dirt or insects are found inside."

After that they would graduate, as the rains passed, to more important jobs. Men of Omoro's age—over 30—rose gradually in rank and responsibility until they acquired the honored status of elders and sat on the Council of Elders.

It was not long before the boys began to understand that the welfare of the group depended upon each one of them—just as the welfare of their tribe would depend on each of them one day. Violations of the rules slowly dwindled to an occasional lapse and, with the decline in beatings, the fear they felt for the *kintango* was gradually replaced by a respect they had felt before only for their fathers.

Still, hardly a day would pass without something new to make Kunta and his mates feel awkward and ignorant all over again. There seemed to be no limit to the things men knew that boys did not. It amazed them to learn, for example, that a rag folded and hung in certain ways near a man's hut would inform other Mandinka men when he planned to return, or that sandals crossed in certain ways outside a man's hut told many things that only other men would understand. But the secret Kunta found the most remarkable of all was *sira kango*, a kind of men's talk in which the sounds of Mandinka words were subtly changed.

Kunta remembered times when he had heard his father say something very rapidly to another man which Kunta had not understood, nor dared to ask about. And now Kunta himself was learning that secret talk. To ask someone where he was going, for instance, one would not say, *"I be to minto?"* but instead would slur quickly, *"Is bes tas mis tos?,"* which no uninformed person could ever follow. Soon Kunta and his mates spoke nearly everything in the secret talk of men.

Ancestral Cities

For the next moon, Kunta and his mates learned how to make war. "You know already," the *kintango* said, "that Mandinkas are the finest warriors."

Famous Mandinka strategies were drawn in the dust by the *kintango*, and the boys re-enacted them in mock battles. Then the boys learned how to make barbed spears tipped with poison. After that it was wrestling, taught by the champion wrestlers of Juffure. And then came instruction in tribal history.

A *griot* arrived, so old that he made the *kintango* seem young. He told the boys, squatted in a semicircle around him, how every *griot* held, buried deep in his mind, the records of the ancestors. "How else could you know of the great deeds of the ancient kings, holy men, hunters and warriors who came hundreds of rains before us?" he asked. "The history of our people is carried to the future in here"—and he tapped his gray head.

He thrilled them until late into the night with stories his own father had passed down to him—about the great black empires that had ruled over Africa hundreds of rains before.

"Long before *toubob* ever put his foot in Africa," the old *griot* said, "there was the empire of ancestral Ghana, in which an entire town was populated with only the king's court. Ghana's most famous king, Kanissaai, had a thousand horses, each of which had three servants and its own urinal made of copper. And each evening," said the *griot*, "when King Kanissaai would emerge from his palace, a thousand fires would be lighted, illuminating all between the heavens and the earth. And the king would sit on a golden porch, surrounded by his horses with their golden reins and saddles, by his dogs with their golden collars, by his guards with their golden shields and swords, and by his princeling sons with golden ornaments in their hair.

"But even Ghana was not the richest black kingdom," he exclaimed. "The very richest, the very oldest of them all was the kingdom of ancient Mali." Mali's enormous wealth came from its far-flung trade routes, its dealings in salt and gold and copper. Caravans of thousands of camels were common sights in such cities as Takedda and Niani, where huge ceremonies and pageants were held almost every day.

"Altogether, Mali was four months of travel long and four months of travel wide," said the *griot*. "And the greatest of all its cities was the fabled Timbuktu." Timbuktu, he told them, had 6000 dwelling houses and many rich mosques. The major center of learning in all Africa, it was populated by thousands of scholars, made even more numerous by a steady parade of visiting wise men seeking to increase their knowledge—so many that some of the biggest merchants sold nothing but parchments and books. "There is not a holy man, not a teacher in the smallest village, whose knowledge has not come at least in part from Timbuktu," said the *griot*.

The next visitor to the compound was a celebrated *jalli kea*, a singing man, who led the boys in songs of great hunters and wise, brave and powerful Mandinka chiefs. Hardly had he left when a famous *moro*—the highest grade of teacher—arrived. He read to them from the Koran, and then from such unheard-of books as the *Taureta La Musa* (the Pentateuch of Moses), the *Zabora Dawidi* (the Psalms of David) and the *Lingeeli La Isa* (the Book of Isaiah). When he had finished, the old man spoke to them of great events from the Christian Koran, which was known as the Holy Bible, of Adam and Eve, of Joseph and his brethren, of David and Solomon.

> He thrilled them with stories about the great black empires that ruled over Africa hundreds of rains before.

In his hut at night, Kunta lay awake thinking how nearly everything they learned tied together. The past seemed with the present, the present with the future, the dead with the living and those yet to live. All lived with Allah. He felt very small—yet very large. This, he thought, is what it means to become a man.

One night, when the moon was high and full in the heavens, the *kintango* helpers ordered the *kafo* to line up shortly after the evening meal.

Was this the moment for which they had waited? Kunta looked around for the *kintango*. His eyes searched the compound and finally found the old man standing at the gate of the *jujuo* just as he was swinging it open wide. The *kintango* turned to them and called out, "Men of Juffure, you will return to your village!"

For a moment they stood rooted. Then they rushed up whooping, and grabbed and hugged their *kintango* and his helpers, who pretended to be offended by such impertinence. Then their thoughts turned homeward.

Capture

When Kunta returned to the village, he found that his father had acquired a hut for him. Kunta would now live by himself, as would each of his *kafo*. Binta still cooked for him, however, and provided his new hut with a pallet, some bowls, a stool and a prayer rug. Kunta skillfully bargained for more household possessions, trading grain and groundnuts grown on a small plot of land assigned to him by the village elders. A young man who tended his crops well and managed his goats wisely could become a man of substance by the time he reached 25 or 30 rains, and begin to think about taking a wife and raising sons of his own.

Every morning he took his prayer rug and fell in with his *kafo* as they walked with bowed heads behind the older men to the mosque. After prayers, Binta brought his breakfast. Then he joined his mates in undertaking their duties, which they performed with a diligence their elders found amusing.

The women could hardly turn around without finding one of the new men demanding to inspect their cooking pots for insects. Rummaging about outside the village fence, they found hundreds of spots where the state of repair failed to measure up to their exacting standards. Fully a dozen of them drew up buckets of well water, tasting carefully from the gourd dipper in hopes of detecting a saltiness or a muddiness or something else unhealthy. They were disappointed, but the fish and turtle that were kept in the well to eat insects were removed anyway and replaced with fresh ones.

At night, when it was his turn, Kunta made his way along the outside of the fence, past the sharp-thorned bushes piled against it and the pointed stakes concealed beneath, to a leafy hiding place that afforded him a view of the surrounding countryside. And here he guarded the village against whatever might threaten it. One night, a full rain since manhood training, Kunta left for the sentry post, taking with him not only his spear and bow, but an ax—for in the morning he intended to select and chop the wood that he would bend and dry into a frame for a drum for the village. Quickly, he climbed the notched pole in whose sturdy fork was built a platform eight feet above the ground.

During the first of his turns alone at these vigils, every shadowy movement of monkey, baboon, hyena or panther had seemed surely to be an enemy. But, after long nights on lookout, Kunta's eyes and ears became so highly trained that he could let them maintain vigilance almost on their own, while his mind explored private thoughts.

Since his new manhood, Kunta had begun to think of taking a very special trip. He meant to put his feet upon that place called Mali where, according to Omoro and his uncles, the ancient Kinte clan had begun, 300 or 400 rains ago. The schoolmaster had drawn a map for him, and estimated that the round trip would take about one moon. Since then, Kunta had many times drawn and studied his planned route on the dirt floor of his hut.

The sudden barking of his *wuolo* dog pushed the thought from his head. Standing on his platform, Kunta whooped and waved his arms at the dark hulks of baboons which had got up the courage to rush from the tall grass adjoining the fields and snatch up a few groundnuts before fleeing back into the bush. Twice more during the night they made forays, growing bolder as dawn approached.

At the first streaks of light in the east, Kunta gathered his weapons and ax, clambered stiffly down to the ground and began limbering up. Then he set off along the *bolong* toward a stand of mangrove trees to find the wood he wanted. He passed through the scattered first trees of the grove, for a thicker growth offered more choice. Leaning his weapons and ax against a warped tree, he moved here, there, his eyes searching for perfect trunks.

The sharp cracking of a twig mixed with a bird's squawk first registered as being merely the *wuolo* dog returning from a chase after a hare—then his reflexes flashed that no dog cracks a twig. Kunta whirled, and, comprehending the rushing, blurred pale face, knew two things that instant: *toubob* and weapons beyond reach.

Steal me...eat me. His foot, lashing up, caught the *toubob* in the belly, but a heavy object from behind grazed his head, then exploded pain in his shoulder. Glimpsing the kicked *toubob* doubling over, Kunta spun, fists flailing. He saw two black *slatee* men, and another *toubob* who was again jerking downward a short, thick club, which Kunta escaped by violently springing aside.

The blacks rushed him, and Kunta—his brain screaming for a weapon, any weapon—leaped into them, clawing, butting, kneeing, gouging. Then, as the three of them went sagging down, another club pounded against his back. A knee smashed over Kunta's kidneys, rocking him with such pain that he gasped; his open mouth met flesh; his teeth clamped, cut and tore. His fingers found a face, and he clawed deeply into an eye as the club hit his head. Dazed, he heard the dog's sudden piteous yelp. Scrambling up, wildly twisting and dodging to escape more clubbing, with blood streaming from his head, he glimpsed one of the *toubob* standing near the brained dog.

Screaming his rage, Kunta went for the *toubob* and, almost choking on the awful *toubob* stink, tried desperately to wrench away the club. Why had he not heard them, sensed them, smelled them? For a split second he clearly saw his family and all the people of Juffure, his mind flashing that if a warrior died bravely, he became a noble ancestor. Everything that had happened to him during his 16 rains seemed to flicker across his consciousness. Raging at his own weakness, he knew he was fighting for more than his life—and then the *toubob's* heavy club squarely met his ear and temple.

Toubob's Canoe

He struggled back to consciousness to find himself gagged and blindfolded, with his wrists tightly bound behind him, his ankles hobbled. He was yanked to his feet, and sharpened sticks jabbed him as he stumbled along. Somewhere on the banks of the *bolong*, he was shoved into a canoe. When the canoe landed, he walked again, until finally that night they reached a camp where he was tied to a thick post and his blindfold removed. Kunta was then left alone. Dawn let him see other captives tied to posts—six men, three maidens and two children, their naked bodies bruised and bloody from being clubbed.

In wild fury, Kunta lunged back and forth trying to burst his bonds. A heavy blow from a club again rendered him senseless. When he woke again, he found himself also naked; his head had been shaved and his body smeared with red palm oil. Soon afterward, two new *toubob* entered the camp, one of them short and stout, his hair white. The *slatees*, now all grins, untied the captives and herded them into a line.

The white-haired one gestured at Kunta. Kunta screamed in terror as a *slatee* behind him wrestled him down to his knees, jerking his head backward. The white-haired *toubob* calmly spread Kunta's trembling lips and studied his teeth. Standing again, Kunta quivered as the *toubob's* fingers explored his eyes, his chest, his belly. Then the fingers grasped his *foto*. Two *slatees* forced Kunta finally to bend himself almost double, and in horror he felt his buttocks being spread wide apart.

> Forced to sit hunched forward, Kunta thrashed and screamed as the hot iron burned into his back.

The white-haired *toubob* similarly inspected the others, one by one—even the private parts of the wailing maidens. Afterward he beckoned a camp *toubob* and jabbed his finger at four men—one of them Kunta—and two maidens.

Kunta struggled and howled with fury as again the *slatees* grabbed him, pushing him into a seated position with his back hunched forward. In terror he could see a *toubob* withdrawing from a fire a long, thin iron. He thrashed and screamed as the iron burned into his back. The camp echoed with the screams of the others who had been selected. Then red palm oil was rubbed over the peculiar, white *LL* shape that Kunta saw on their backs.

A few days later they were hobbling along tied together in a line, the *slatees'* clubs falling on anyone who balked. Kunta's back and shoulders were bruised and bleeding when, late that night, the captives were put in canoes and paddled through the darkness. When Kunta finally perceived the dark hulk looming up ahead in the night, he raged anew against his bonds. Heavy club blows rained down on him as the canoe bumped against the side of the dark object, and he heard above him the exclamations of many *toubob*. Helpless to resist the ropes looped around him, he was half pushed, half pulled up a rope ladder.

In the shadowy, yellowish light cast by lanterns, he glimpsed the short, stout *toubob* with the white hair calmly making marks in a book. Then Kunta was guided, stumbling, down narrow steps into a place of pitch blackness. He smelled an incredible stink, and his ears heard many men's moans of anguish. As he was shoved down, flat on his back, he felt briefly that he was dreaming—and then lapsed mercifully into unconsciousness.

"Allah, Help Me!"

When he awoke, Kunta wondered if he had gone mad. He lay shuddering, chained down naked between two other men in a pitch darkness full of heat and stink and a nightmarish bedlam of weeping, praying and vomiting. A rat's thick, furry body brushed his cheek. As he lunged upward, his head bumped dizzyingly against a ceiling scarcely a foot above him. Gasping with pain, he slumped back, wishing that he might die.

I am trapped like a leopard in a snare! Kunta fought back panic. He guessed that many men must be shackled on the rough plank shelves in the foul darkness, and that some of them were down on another level below where he lay. They spoke in a babble of tongues—Fulani, Serere, Wolof and Mandinka. The man on his right, to whom he was shackled at wrist and ankle, muttered angrily to himself in Wolof. On his left, there was only a steady moaning.

Kunta lay for a while, sobbing, his mind numbed. Though he could not get onto his knees, and he was unaware of which direction was east, he closed his eyes and prayed, beseeching Allah's help.

In the darkness of the big vessel, only the occasional opening of the deck hatch enabled Kunta to tell if it was day or night. Usually, when the hatch opened, four shadowy *toubob* figures would descend, two with lanterns and whips, the others pushing tubs of food along the aisleways. They would thrust tin pans of the food up onto the filth between the men shackled together. Kunta defiantly clamped his jaws shut, preferring to starve to death—until the aching of his stomach made his hunger almost as terrible as his other pains.

Shortly after feeding time, Kunta's ears picked up a sound vibrating through the planks over his head, as if many feet were dash-

ing about. Then came the sound of some heavy object creaking slowly upward. Kunta lay frozen, gradually sensing a slow, rocking motion. Then terror clawed into his vitals as he realized, "This place is moving. It's taking us away."

Abruptly, the men in the hold went into a frenzy of screaming, banging their heads against the planks, rattling their chains. "Allah," Kunta shrieked into the bedlam, "hear me! Help me!" And when his voice was gone from shouting, his mind screamed out in rage and helplessness, *"Toubob fa!"* ("Kill *toubob*!") After a while he lay back limply, sobbing.

The next time the hatch rasped open, something the *kintango* had once said flashed into his mind: *Warriors must eat well to have great strength*. Weakness for lack of food would not let him kill *toubob*. And so this time when the tin pan was thrust up next to him, his fingers dipped into the thick mush of ground corn boiled with palm oil. He swallowed painfully until he could feel the food like a lump in his belly. Then he vomited—and vomited again.

Ankle shackles were used to immobilize the captives during the transatlantic crossing to servitude in North and South America and the Caribbean.

Dance of Death

As the days passed in the hold, vomit and feces gathered on the moaning, shackled men. In the filth, the lice multiplied by the millions until they swarmed all over the hold. Finally, eight naked *toubob* came down through the hatchway cursing loudly. Instead of food they carried long-handled hoes and large tubs. In teams of two they moved along the aisle, thrusting their hoes up onto the shelves and scraping the mess into their tubs. But when they had finished, there was no difference in the choking stench of the hold.

Not long afterward, many *toubob* descended. Kunta guessed that there must be 20 clumping down the hatch steps, some carrying whips and guns, the metal weapons of fire and smoke he had heard about when men spoke of *toubob* in Juffure. A knot of fear grew in Kunta's belly as he heard strange clicking sounds, then heavy rattlings. Suddenly, his shackled right ankle began jerking. He was being released. Why? Then the *toubob* started shouting and lashing with their whips. In different tongues, all the men around Kunta were beseeching the *toubob* not to eat them.

One after another, pairs of men, still shackled at the wrists, went thumping off their shelves into the aisles. Kunta's long-unused muscles tightened with pain. He and his shacklemate were shoved and kicked along in the darkness toward the hatchway steps. As he stumbled up onto the deck, the sunlight hit him with the blinding force of a hammer. Fumbling ahead, he opened his cracked lips, gulping in the salty air. Then his lungs convulsed and, close to choking, he collapsed on the deck with his Wolof shacklemate.

> He was chained to the others and crying in agony as the salt water hit him, stinging like fire in his whip cuts.

In the light, the *toubob* looked even more wild and sickly pale than below, their long hair in colors of yellow or black or red, some of them even with hair around their mouths and under their chins. Some had ugly scars from knives, or a hand, eye or limb missing, and the backs of many were crisscrossed with deep scars from whips. A lot of the *toubob* were spaced along the rails, holding cutlasses or guns. Turning about, Kunta saw that a high barricade of bamboo extended completely across the width of the huge craft. Showing through its center was the black barrel of a cannon.

For the first time, Kunta observed his Wolof shacklemate in the light. Like himself, the man was crusted with filth, and pus was oozing from where the *LL* shape had been burned into his back. Looking about, Kunta saw more suffering men.

Now they were chained together by their ankle shackles in groups of ten and doused with buckets of sea water. *Toubob* with long-handled brushes then scrubbed the naked men. Kunta cried in agony as the salt water hit him, stinging like fire in his whip cuts, cried out again as the bristles tore the scabs from his back and shoulders. Bleeding from his wounds, Kunta and his shacklemates were herded back to the center of the deck, where they flopped down in huddled terror.

The sudden cries of women brought the chained men jerking upright. About 20 of them came running, naked and unchained, from behind the barricade. With a flooding rage, Kunta perceived all of the *toubob* leering at their nakedness. Then a *toubob* near the rail began pulling out and pushing in some peculiar thing in his hands which made a wheezing music. A second man beat on a drum. Other *toubob* began jumping up and down in short hops, keeping time to the drumbeats and gesturing that the petrified men in chains should jump in the same manner.

"Jump!" shrieked the oldest woman suddenly, in Mandinka. "Jump now to kill *toubob*!" She began jumping up and down, her arms darting in the movements of the warriors' dance. When her meaning sank home, one after another shackled pair of naked men commenced a weak, stumbling hopping, their chains clanking and jangling against the deck. Kunta felt his legs rubbery under him, vaguely hearing the singing of the women. Then he became aware that in their singing the women were saying that the *toubob* took them into the dark corners of the vessel and made use of them. *"Toubob fa!"* they shouted, jumping up and down in a frenzy, while the grinning *toubob* clapped their hands with pleasure.

"We Must Be One Village!"

Chained back down in his place in the stinking hold, Kunta gradually noticed a low murmuring of voices in the darkness. He and his Wolof shacklemate had occasionally exchanged cautious whispers, picking up words in the other's tongue, much as toddling children of the first *kafo* learned their early words. But now that the men had actually seen each other in the daylight, there was a new quality to the whispers, as if there was between them for the first time a sense of brotherhood.

As their understanding improved, many questions were asked in the darkness. "How long have we been here?" brought a rash of guesses, until the question finally reached a man who had been able to keep a count of daylights through a small air vent. He said that he had counted 18 days since the great canoe had begun moving. Some asked if there were others in the hold from the same village.

One day, Kunta nearly burst with excitement when the Wolof relayed the question, "Is one here from Juffure village?"

"Kunta Kinte!" he whispered breathlessly. He waited tensely during the hour it took for a response to return: "Yes, that was the name. I heard the drums—his village was grieving." Kunta dissolved into sobs, his mind streaming before him pictures of his family weeping and mourning their son, Kunta Kinte, gone forever.

How could the *toubob* on the big canoe be attacked and killed? How many were there? Days of questions and replies sought the answers. In the end the most useful information came from the women's singing as the men danced in their chains on deck. They said about 30 *toubob* remained on the craft, after five dead ones had been sewn into white cloth and thrown into the endless blue water.

Arguments arose as to how to kill the *toubob*. Some wanted to attack the next time they were allowed on deck. Others felt it would be wiser to watch and wait. Bitter disagreements grew in the stinking darkness, until one day the voice of an elderly man rang out: "Hear me! Though we are of different tribes and tongues, we must be together in this place as one village! And we must be as one behind our leader!" Murmurings of approval spread in the hold.

One fierce-looking Wolof led the argument that the *toubob* should be attacked immediately. On deck, everyone had seen this man dancing wildly in his chains while baring his sharply filed teeth at the *toubob*, who clapped for him because they thought he was grinning.

The group that believed in watchful preparation was led by a gloomy, whip-scarred Fula. Kunta had no doubt that the fierce Wolof could have led an army, but he joined in choosing the Fula as leader. Everyone knew that a Fula would spend years, even his entire life, bitterly avenging a serious wrong.

Soon they were herded on deck again, where, in obedience to the Fula, they tried to act happy in order to relax the *toubob's* guard. Still, Kunta worried that the *toubob* might sense the growing difference in the way they danced, for now they could not keep their bodies from reflecting what was deep in their minds. But the grinning *toubob* appeared to remain unsuspecting.

One day on deck, Kunta stood rooted in astonishment, watching thousands of fish fly over the water like silvery birds, when suddenly he heard an animal-like scream. Whirling, he saw the fierce Wolof snatch a gun from a *toubob*. Swinging it like a club, he sent the *toubob's* brains flying. Then, bellowing in rage, he clubbed the

others swarming toward him, until a cutlass flashed and the Wolof's head was lopped off. Then the big black barrel of the cannon exploded with a thunderous roar of heat and smoke just above the shackled men, and they screamed and sprawled on top of each other in terror.

Amid shouts, the *toubob* rushed the shackled men back toward the hatch with their guns and cutlasses. Almost before they realized it, the men found themselves again below, chained in their dark places as the hatch cover slammed down. For a long while, no one dared even to whisper. Bitterly, Kunta wondered why the signal to attack had not been given. From the gradually louder muttering sounds around him, it became evident that many men shared his thoughts. Soon word was passed from the Fula that the attack would come the next time they were all on deck being washed.

But, that night, Kunta heard a new sound from on deck. He guessed that strong winds must be making the great white cloths above flap more than usual. Then there was another sound, as if rain were pelting onto the deck. The big canoe began violently, jerkily rolling, and the men cried out in agony as their shoulders, elbows and buttocks, already festered and bleeding, were ground down on the rough boards beneath.

On the edge of consciousness, Kunta became dimly aware of the

Pen, ink and wash illustration of the *Southwell Frigate*, a British slave ship that traded on Africa's west coast, c. 1760.

sound of water spilling down heavily into the hold. There was a clomping of feet, the sound of something like heavy cloth being dragged across the deck, and the noise of falling water lessened as the openings were covered. But now the heat and stench were trapped entirely within the hold. Gagging, Kunta gasped for breath.

That night, he revived on deck, jerkily breathing fresh sea air. By lantern light he saw *toubob* stumbling up through the open hatchway, slipping in vomit, dragging limp, shackled forms onto the deck and dumping them down near him. The great canoe was still pitching heavily, and the white-haired chief *toubob* had difficulty keeping his balance as he examined the bodies closely. Sometimes then, cursing bitterly, he would bark an order, and other *toubob* would drag a limp form over to the rail and dump it into the ocean.

These had died in the hell below. Kunta envied them.

Delirium

By dawn, the weather had cleared. Looking dully around him, Kunta saw men lying on deck, many of them convulsing. The chief *toubob* was now moving among the chained men, applying salve and powder to their wounds. He opened the mouths of some of the men and forced down their throats something from a black bottle. When the *toubob* put grease on him, Kunta looked away. He would rather have felt a lash than the pale hands against his skin.

The next days were a twilight of pain and sickness. Lying below deck in his filth, Kunta did not know if they had been in the stinking belly of the *toubob* canoe for several moons, or even as long as a rain—for the man was now dead who had counted the days. Kunta's shacklemate had died, too. The *toubob* came, detached him from Kunta and dragged his stiff body away. Kunta lay limp with fear and shock: *"Toubob fa!"* he screamed into the darkness. But he was too sick and weak to care much about killing anyone anymore.

It was at first only a few of the men in the hold who began to make terrible new cries of pain. Their bowels had begun to drain a mixture of clotted blood and thick, yellow mucus. The *toubob* bringing the food, upon first smelling and glimpsing the putrid discharge, displayed great agitation. Minutes later, the chief *toubob* descended. Despite the camphor bag clamped between his teeth, he was soon gagging. Gesturing sharply, he had the newly sick men taken up through the hatch.

But it was of no use, for the contagion of the bloody flux moved swiftly. Severe pains in the head and back, a roasting fever and a shivering of the body were already in most of the men. When Kunta felt the awful, hot compulsion in his bowels, his cries of pain joined the increasing bedlam in the hold. In delirium he cried out the names of his father and grandfather: "Omoro—Omar the second Caliph, third after Muhammad the Prophet! Kairaba—Kairaba means peace!"

Each day now, the shackled sufferers were dragged up on deck into the fresh air, while *toubob* took down buckets of boiling vinegar and tar to fumigate the hold. Yet every day someone else died and was thrown overboard—sometimes a *toubob*.

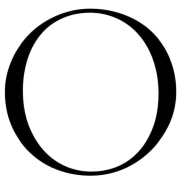

ne day when Kunta got up into the light and air, he dimly noticed that the great white sheets on the tall poles were drooping. It was hard to see; Kunta's once keen eyes were now gummy with some rheumy, yellowish matter—but the big canoe seemed to be almost motionless on a layer of gold-colored seaweed. The ship had entered the Sargasso Sea and was becalmed.

No more lashings now fell on the men's backs, and they were given more food and water. As much as 100 pounds of flying fish were lured aboard each night with lanterns, and the flesh added to the cornmeal. Still, the time finally came when Kunta could no longer even eat without help. The shreds of muscles in his arms refused to lift his hands for him to claw into the tin food pan. A *toubob* put a hollow tube into his mouth and poured gruel down his gullet.

At last the breeze freshened. Soon the big canoe was again cutting through the water with a foaming sound and, as the days passed, Kunta sensed a kind of excitement among the *toubob*. One morning they seemed particularly elated as they rushed into the hold and helped the crawling, scrambling men up through the hatch. Blinking in the early-morning light, Kunta saw the other *toubob* all wildly laughing, cheering and pointing. Between the scabbed, festering backs of the lice-encrusted men, Kunta kept squinting with his rheumy eyes—and then he was petrified.

Blurry in the distance, there was unmistakably some piece of Allah's earth again.

Land of Toubabo Doo

Capt. Thomas Davies, with Cape Henry, Virginia, now in sight, retired to his cabin and began reviewing the whole voyage, his first as captain after years as a mate on slave ships. It was, moreover, the maiden voyage of his vessel, the *Lord Ligonier*. Built not quite two years before, in colonial New England, she was 68 feet long and 150 tons.

Drawing a document from his desk, he looked over his sailing orders: "We request the taking of only prime, able-bodied, well-formed, healthy, strong Negroes...and secondly any other items of cargo such as a lack of slaves may make room for."

Being as candid as possible with himself, the white-haired captain could find no major mistakes that he had made. The storm, the flux, the death of 42 Negroes and several crewmen, he could see but as the will of God. The 98 slaves remaining would bring a huge profit to the ship's owners. His personal salary called for $1200, plus a bonus of £6 for every slave delivered.

He had first sailed the *Lord Ligonier* from Annapolis to Graves-end, England, ballasted with a cargo of rum, which was easily sold. With part of the profits he bought 450 sets of wrist and ankle shackles; six dozen 20-foot lengths of thick chain; two branding irons with the ship's initials; and a plentiful supply of colorful, cheap goods for trading on the coast of Africa.

With additional crewmen, the *Lord Ligonier* sailed for Africa in July 1766. On her way, the ship was prepared to receive slaves. The carpenter raised ventilation openings on the deck and built long plank shelves in the hold. On these, with ruler and paint, he marked the 16-inch width allowed for each slave. The gunner made cartridges for the swivel guns; the mate plaited from strips of rawhide a supply of cat-o'-nine-tails. Sixty-eight days later—a disappointingly slow passage—Davies sighted land, entered the mouth of the Gambia River and paid a tax to the black King of Essau, who ruled the territory. Then he proceeded upriver and anchored off British-owned Fort St. James, which shipped up to 2000 slaves a year.

Before doing anything else, Davies sent men ashore to purchase mangrove thatching to build a barricade deckhouse. One wall would have an opening for mounting a swivel gun in case the slaves tried mutiny at sea. Then he visited some of the other ships in the harbor. Their captains warned him that prices were high—£25 apiece for prime slaves. And the black *slatees* would no longer take trinkets for their help; they demanded money. Captain Davies determined not to pay ransom prices for a quick cargo. He would patiently buy one black at a time, meticulously examining and selecting the individual Negroes who would bring top money in Annapolis.

Afterward he went to inspect some slaves. He bought two good specimens, a young male and female, endured their screaming as one of the new branding irons seared the identifying *LL* between their shoulders. In his log, when finally he put them on the ship, he made the traditional entry for the first male and female: "Adam and Eve on board."

Working with independent dealers, he began to acquire the slaves he sought. But, as the months passed, he increasingly had to turn to dealing with the larger, more expensive slave factories. There were 13 on the Gambia River, usually run by a degraded former ship captain and manned by *slatee* guards. The factories bought—at wholesale prices—entire coffles of slaves captured in village raids.

By the end of May 1767, he still had only 118 slaves. There was space for 200 on board—males in the hold, women and children in the barricade house. But a number of ships, arriving after the *Lord Ligonier*, had already departed with second-rate cargoes of slaves. Word of their quick round trip would travel fast. The captain knew his owners must be wondering what was keeping him so long.

Finally, on July 5, having bought 22 more slaves and filled the ship's empty spaces with 1250 elephant's teeth, 3700 pounds of beeswax, 800 pounds of cotton and 32 ounces of gold, Captain Davies set sail. He reached Cape Henry the third week of September.

> The 98 slaves still alive should bring at least $600 apiece— a gross of about $58,000, since the children would bring less.

In his cabin, Davies continued figuring. The 98 slaves still alive should bring at least $600 apiece—a gross of about $58,000, since the children would bring less—and the incidental cargo another $1000. Even after paying off the crew (at $5 a month), sundry expenses and the cost of the ship, his owners would have $36,000 clear profit. He had not done badly for them. They should volunteer him a good bonus beyond what he was owed. A few more voyages and he could comfortably retire—God willing.

As Kunta squinted at the still blurry land, his whole body began to shake. Sweat glistened on his forehead. Then tears flooded everything into a gray, swimming mist as a deep sense of foreboding came over him. These *toubob* really did have some place to put their feet upon—the land of *toubabo doo*—and deep within himself Kunta knew that whatever would come next was going to be yet worse than what lay behind.

Auction in Annapolis

The small ship, the *Lord Ligonier*, arrived off the coast of Virginia in September 1767, and entered the strong current of Chesapeake Bay for the four-day journey to its home port of Annapolis. Belowdecks, in a misery of filth, lice and disease, was a cargo of 98 blacks, the weakened remnants of the 140 slaves who had been on board when the ship sailed from Gambia, West Africa.

Down in the stinking darkness, trembling with new fears now that they knew they were approaching the land of the *toubob*— the white man—the chained men did not open their mouths. Their silence let them hear more clearly the ship's timbers creaking, the muted *ssss* of the sea against the hull and the dulled clumpings of *toubob* feet on the deck overhead. During the two months and three weeks at sea, the ship's countless motions had rubbed the men's weight against the rough planking on which they lay until their buttocks and shoulders were badly ulcerated and seeping blood.

On one of the shelves allotted to the blacks lay 17-year-old Kunta Kinte. In his native village of Juffure it was an honored name, the name of his grandfather, a holy man who had earned lasting fame by praying to Allah unstintingly for five days and nights to end a drought, thus saving Juffure from famine.

Kunta's back, like the others', was raw from the voyage and had been deeply branded, before departing, with the ship's initials, *LL*. Like the others, he had suffered terribly from the whips of the *toubob* and from a host of diseases and parasites. And, like most of the others, he had prayed constantly to Allah for an end to this time of horror.

On the fourth day after land was sighted, the blacks were yanked roughly to the deck for a final scrubbing with coarse brushes, then were rubbed with oil until they shone. When the ship finally docked, the weak, sick, fear-numbed black men were driven under steadily cracking whips down the gangway onto the *toubob* earth. The impulse to escape surged wildly in Kunta, but *toubob* whips kept his chained line under tight control.

As they shuffled in single file alongside a gesturing, jeering

> **TO BE SOLD** on board the Ship *Bance-Yland*, on tuesday the 6th of *May* next, at *Afhley-Ferry*; a choice cargo of about 250 fine healthy
>
> **NEGROES,** juft arrived from the Windward & Rice Coaft.
> —The utmoft care has already been taken, and fhall be continued, to keep them free from the leaft danger of being infected with the SMALL-POX, no boat having been on board, and all other communication with people from *Charles-Town* prevented.
> *Auftin, Laurens, & Appleby.*
>
> *N. B.* Full one Half of the above Negroes have had the SMALL-POX in their own Country.

crowd, he glimpsed finely clothed *toubob* watching the chained blacks with expressions of loathing. He saw incredulously what was surely a she *toubob*, with hair the color of straw. And he saw two black men, unmistakably a Mandinka tribesman and a Serere. They walked behind a *toubob*, their faces expressionless. Kunta's mind reeled: how could blacks docilely follow behind *toubob*?

The men were taken to a large square house of burnt mud with bars set into the few open spaces along the sides. In a large room, the wrists and ankles of Kunta and his mates were locked in thick iron cuffs, which were chained to bolts set in the walls. Terrified, Kunta huddled down on the cold earthen floor and beseeched Allah to save him.

After darkness fell—Kunta could see stars through one of the iron-barred spaces near him—he became more composed, and thoughts began to flicker through his mind like shadows in a dream. Wincing, he remembered the carelessness which had led to his capture as he searched outside his village for a piece of wood with which to make a drum; the nightmarish trip down the waters of the *bolong* to the place where the big *toubob* canoe waited. Although he did not wish to bring even their memory to this hated

A newspaper ad from the 1780s announcing the sale, near Charleston, South Carolina, of people captured on the west coast of Africa.

place, he could not help but think of his father, Omoro, and his mother, Binta, and his three younger brothers. And then he was sobbing.

It was nearly dawn, Kunta sensed, when there came into his head the sharp voice of his teacher, the *kintango*: "A man is wise to study and learn from the animals." Was this some message from Allah? Kunta was like an animal in a trap. The animals which he had known to escape their traps had not raged within, but quietly conserved their strength until a moment of carelessness gave them the chance to explode in flight. So, too, must Kunta appear to the *toubob* to have given up hope.

Through the small, barred space, Kunta counted six daylights and six nights. Three times each day a strange black man brought food. Kunta forced it down, knowing it would give him strength. Then, after the seventh morning meal, four *toubob* entered. Two stayed just inside the doorway, holding guns and clubs. The others unlocked the iron cuffs. In a chained line of six men, Kunta was shoved out into the bright sunlight.

> Kunta was pushed toward the platform. "Prime—young and supple," the auctioneer shouted.

"Just picked out of the trees! … Bright as monkeys!" A shouting man was standing on a low wooden platform, addressing a crowd. Kunta's nose rebelled at the heavy *toubob* stink as he and his mates were jerked through the mass of people. Then Kunta was unchained from the others and pushed toward the platform.

"Prime—young and supple!" The *toubob* was shouting again. Numb with terror, Kunta could scarcely breathe. Other *toubob* were moving in closely around him. With short sticks and whip butts they thrust apart his compressed lips, exposing his clenched teeth. They prodded him all over, on his back, his chest, his genitals. Then they stepped back and, amid the babbling of the shouting man, began to make their own strange cries: "Three hundred dollars!" "Three fifty!"

There were more strange sounds, and then Kunta heard, "Eight hundred fifty!" When no other calls came, the shouting one unhitched Kunta's chain and pulled him toward a *toubob* who had stepped forward. He then saw behind the *toubob* a black one with distinct Wolof-tribe features. *My brother, you come from my country.* … But the black one seemed not even to notice Kunta. He pulled hard on the chain so that Kunta came stumbling after him, and they began moving through the crowd. They stopped at a kind of box on

Interior view of a slave pen in Alexandria, Virginia, between 1861 and 1869.

wheels behind a large animal—the first horse Kunta had ever seen. The black one grabbed Kunta about the hips and boosted him onto the floor of the box.

Kunta heard the free end of his chain click into something at the front of the box. The black one and the *toubob* climbed up onto a seat, and the horse began pulling the box away, away from the big water which, far off where the sun rose, touched the land where Kunta had been born. Again into his head came a voice, this time of a village elder sitting beside a fire in Juffure: "No man really knows the land of *toubob*, for no one has ever returned from there to describe it."

Flight

As the box creaked along, Kunta raised himself up and could see what he guessed were *toubob* fields. In one he recognized stalks of corn, the ears already picked; in another, he could distinguish the figures of black workers with a *toubob* standing over them. They passed a line of about 20 black men, chained together by wrist cuffs and guarded by a *toubob* on a horse. The men were singing mournfully, but the sounds made no sense to Kunta.

At dusk, the rolling box turned off onto a small road and drew up before a large white house. Kunta saw several black people there, and hope surged in him when the *toubob* walked off toward the house. Would these black ones free him now? But they did nothing, and he wondered with a burst of rage what kind of blacks these were who acted as the goats of the *toubob*.

Kunta slept on the ground chained to a stake. In the morning, he had barely time to make his dawn prayer to Allah, bowing to the east, before they were on the road again. The sights and sounds were similar to those of the previous day. Twice more, always distant from the road, he saw large white *toubob* houses; nearby were mud and log huts where Kunta guessed the blacks lived.

fter the sun set on the third day, the box turned off the main road. Squinting through the moonlit darkness, Kunta could see the ghostly whiteness of another big house. Soon the box came to a stop. The *toubob* got down, spoke to the black one and went into the house. The box creaked on toward some small huts and stopped again. Kunta heard the click of the thing which had held his chain. The black one got down, came to the edge of the box and with one powerful arm levered Kunta up over the side to the ground.

In that instant the smaller Kunta exploded upward, his hands clamping about the black one's throat like the jaws of a hyena. The black one gave a hoarse sound; then he was pounding and clawing at Kunta's face and arms. Kunta's hands clamped tighter still until the man stumbled backward and went limp.

Springing up, Kunta fled wildly toward where he could see, in the moonlight, a distant forest. He kept low, his flailing legs crashing through frosted cornstalks. His long-unused muscles screamed with pain, but the cold, rushing air felt good, and he grunted with the pleasure of being free again. He reached the forest and plunged in, stumbling through brambles and vines, deeper and deeper, until suddenly he burst upon low brush. He saw with a shock that he had come to another wide field and another white house.

He ran back into the thickest part of the woods, his bare feet cut and bleeding. Then, on all fours, he crawled into deep undergrowth and passed the night there. As dawn came he kneeled and, facing the east, prayed to Allah.

Kunta first heard the deep baying of the dogs at a distance. The sound became louder and more insistent, and behind the baying he soon detected the shouting of men. Wildly, he went plunging through the brambles. But when he heard a *toubob* gun, he panicked and fell in the tangled briers.

Two dogs came crashing through the brush, snarling and biting at him. He tried to fight them off with his hands, at the same time sliding away from them like a crab. He heard men yelling from the edge of the thicket. Again the gun fired; the growling dogs backed off.

Several men with knives and clubs rushed toward him. Kunta recognized the black one whom he had choked. He looked murderous. Behind him were *toubob*, their faces reddish and sweating from exertion. The black one came forward, uncoiling a rope. A heavy blow to Kunta's head sent him into numbing shock. His arms were bound to his sides, and he was roughly hauled by a rope out of the forest and across a field to a tree. There the rope was thrown over a limb, and the black one pulled on it until Kunta's feet barely touched the ground. A *toubob* whip lashed against his back. He writhed under the pain, refusing to cry out, but each stroke felt as if it were tearing him in half. He began screaming, the lashing went on—and he passed out.

When consciousness returned, Kunta found himself spread-eagled, chained by his ankles and wrists to four stout poles in the corners of a small hut. The slightest movement brought excruciating pain, so he lay completely still, his face wet with sweat, his breath coming in shallow gasps. He berated himself for not waiting longer—as the wise animal would have waited. He had failed, he told himself, because he had tried to escape too soon.

The Lost Tribe

On the fifth morning, shortly after the wakeup horn had blown, the black one entered carrying two thick iron cuffs connected by a short chain. Bending down, he fastened the cuffs around Kunta's ankles. Only then did he unfasten Kunta's other chains. Roughly jerking him to his feet, he began jabbing at Kunta's chest with his finger, uttering strange sounds: "You—Toby!" Kunta did not understand. He stared at him dumbly.

The black one tapped on his own chest. "I Samson!" he

A slave family in the cotton fields of a plantation near Savannah, Georgia, c. 1860s.

exclaimed. His finger poked again at Kunta. "You Toby! Massa say you name Toby!"

His meaning slowly registered on Kunta, and he felt a flooding rage. He wanted to shout at the black one, "I am Kunta Kinte, the first son of Omoro, who is the son of the holy man Kairaba Kunta Kinte!"

The black one led Kunta outside to a large tin bucket that held water for him to wash in. Then he threw him some *toubob* garments to cover his chest and legs, and a hat of yellowish straw. Following the man called Samson, Kunta was taken on a quick tour of his surroundings. The blacks lived in ten huts, arranged in two rows, made of logs and chinked with a reddish mud.

In one of them he was given food by an old woman. Then Samson motioned with his head toward the distant fields. He walked off and Kunta followed, hobbling in his iron shackles. As they approached, he could see black men slashing down cornstalks while the women and younger men gathered them up.

In the field, a *toubob* rode up on his big horse and briefly exchanged words with Samson, who picked up a long, stout knife and slashed down about a dozen stalks. Turning about, he made motions for Kunta to pick them up. The *toubob* jerked his horse closer, his whip cocked. Enraged at his helplessness, Kunta bent down and began gathering the stalks.

In the days that followed, Kunta forced himself to do what was wanted of him. But behind his blank expression he missed nothing. He learned that he was in a place called Spotsylvania County, Virginia. The *toubob* who had brought him to this place was called "massa" by the black ones. In the big white house where the massa lived, there was a she *toubob* called "missis." Kunta had seen her once at a distance, a bony creature the color of a toad's underbelly. In the fields, Kunta learned, there was "corn," and when all the stalks had been cut and piled they then picked large round things the blacks called "punkins." They were put on a "wagon" and taken to a "barn."

But the thing which most interested and mystified him was the attitude of the other blacks. In the evenings, Kunta would sit down just inside the doorway of his hut with his legs stuck out to reduce the pain of the cuffs, while the other adults quietly seated themselves on wooden stools around a fire before the old cooking woman's hut. The sight filled him with a melancholy memory of the night fires in Juffure.

Usually the woman who cooked at the big house would speak first. She mimicked things said by the massa and missis, and Kunta heard the others all but choking to suppress their laughter lest it carry across to the big white house.

But then the laughter would subside, and the blacks simply talked among themselves. Kunta heard the helpless, haunted tone of some and the bitter anger of others, even when he could not know what they were saying. Finally the talking would die away as one of the women began singing and all joined in. Kunta did not understand the words, but he sensed deep sadness in the melodies.

They were heathen, pagan blacks—they even ate the flesh of the filthy swine—yet they did some things which were unmistakably African, and Kunta could tell that they were totally unaware of it themselves. All his life he had heard in Juffure the same sounds of spontaneous exclamations, punctuated with the same gestures and facial expressions. The way they moved their bodies was identical, and the way they laughed when they were together.

How had these people come to be in this place? Kunta could not fathom what had happened to them to so destroy their minds that they acted resigned, complacent, grinning at the massa and the "oberseer."

Perhaps, he thought, it was because they had never known a home village in Africa. They had been born black in this place. They were as a lost tribe.

Kunta reflected on all that he saw and heard and could neither understand nor accept it. And each night before sleep came he swore to his forefathers that he would escape; that he would die before he became like these black ones here.

Cruel Choice

Kunta's left ankle finally became so infected from the chafing of the iron that the overseer had the cuffs removed. With his iron bonds gone and unable to abide waiting, Kunta stole away that night, but Samson caught him only a short distance from his hut.

Kunta was pummeled and kicked, but not whipped or shackled. Soon he fled again after what the blacks called "snow" had fallen from the sky. The overseer caught up with him on one of the big farm horses by following the marks he made in the filmy whiteness. This time he was whipped and chained down. Yet he knew that as soon as the opportunity came, he would try again.

The moons went by, the fields were plowed, and spring planting began with seeds of various kinds, mostly of corn and something called "cotton." Kunta was unshackled, and he did what he was ordered to do, biding his time, chopping away weeds from the plants. As the harvesting began, Kunta noticed that wagons appeared more and more frequently on the distant roads, carrying the cotton to market. It came to him: the way to escape was to hide in a wagon which would carry him far away.

His head burst with working out the details of the plan. He ruled out the cotton wagons of the farm on which he worked; someone was always watching. It must be one of the wagons which he had seen far off, moving along the main road.

One night, on the pretext of going to the outhouse, he studied the road. The flickering light of lanterns inching along told him that the wagons traveled in darkness as well as daylight. Another night he was able to kill a rabbit with a rock; he dried it as he had learned to do in Juffure. Then he honed to sharpness an old, rusty knife blade he had found and carved a wooden handle for it. He also made a *safo* charm. It had a cock's feather to attract the spirits, a horse's hair for strength and a bird's wishbone for success, all wrapped and sewed inside a square of burlap.

One evening he pushed into a pocket the dried pieces of rabbit and tied the *safo* tightly about his upper right arm. Listening tensely through his hut's door, he heard the familiar night routine of the other blacks. Finally their mournful singing ended. When he was sure they were asleep, Kunta grasped his homemade knife and slipped out.

Seeing and sensing no one about, he bent low and began running. Where the farm road met the big road he huddled down into a thick growth of brush. Soon he heard a wagon. It seemed forever before its flickering light even came into view, but finally it was directly opposite Kunta. Two figures sat in front, but there was no rear lookout. Teeth clenched, muscles quivering, Kunta burst from the brush, hunkered down behind the squeaking wagon and—as it bumped over a rough spot—clawed over the tailboard.

The night was his friend, and he burrowed into the cotton and rode undetected. But when dawn touched the sky he left the wagon and quickly disappeared into the underbrush.

The dew that sprinkled him felt good, and he swung his knife as if it were weightless, working deep into what he assured himself was a large area of forest. In the afternoon he chewed a piece of the dried rabbit with water. He plunged on until after sundown, when he made a bed of leaves and grass.

In the morning, he continued on. He did not know where he was or where he was going—only that he must escape. If he followed the way to where the sun rose, it should lead him back, in time, to the big canoe. And then? Kunta felt a growing uncertainty and fright. He prayed often to Allah and fingered his *safo*.

For four days he traveled through the forest, hearing nothing but toads and birds and insects. But on the morning of the fifth day he was awakened by the sound he feared most—the baying of dogs. He sprang up and began running—then realized he had forgotten his knife. Dashing back, he searched desperately among the vines and leaves, but could not find it. Steadily the baying came closer. He found a rock about the size of his fist and ran wildly, tripping, falling.

The bloodhounds cornered him early the next morning. Too exhausted to run farther, he waited, with his back against a tree. His left hand clutched a stout branch, and his right was like a claw about the rock. The dogs stayed out of range of his makeshift club, baying and slavering, until two *toubob* appeared on horses. Kunta had never seen them before. They were professional slave catchers.

The older of the two men dismounted and walked toward him, a club in one hand, a whip in the other. As the *toubob* came closer, Kunta hurled the rock. He heard the *toubob* shout and saw blood running down his head.

Now both men approached him with guns and clubs. He knew from their faces that he would die and he did not care. They clubbed him nearly senseless, but still he writhed and shrieked as they tore his clothes off and roped him to a tree. Kunta steeled himself to be beaten to death.

Then the bleeding *toubob* halted abruptly. A look came on his face, almost a smile, and he spoke briefly to the younger one, who grinned and nodded. The younger one went back to his horse, unlashed an ax from the saddle and gave it to his companion.

The bleeding one stood before Kunta. He pointed to Kunta's testicles, then to the hunting knife in his belt. He pointed to Kunta's foot, and then to the ax in his hand.

Kunta understood. He was being given a choice: his foot or his testicles. Something deep in his marrow shouted that a man, to be a man, must have sons. Involuntarily, his hands flew down to cover his genitals.

The *toubob* were grinning. One of them pushed a log under Kunta's right foot, and the other tied the foot to the tree so tightly that all of Kunta's raging could not free it. Then the bleeding *toubob* picked up the ax.

Kunta screamed and thrashed. The ax whipped up, then down, and severed the front half of his foot. As the blood spurted out, Kunta's body went limp.

A Woman Named Bell

When he regained consciousness, he was in some new place—a hut. He was tied down by the wrists and ankles, with his right foot propped against something soft.

Slave quarters and wood house on the grounds of an estate in Maryland.

A tall *toubob* came in carrying a small black bag. Kunta had never seen this one before. Brushing aside the flies, the *toubob* bent down alongside Kunta and did something that brought such spasms of pain that Kunta shrieked like a woman. "Bell!" the man called out, and a short, powerfully built black woman came inside bringing water in a tin container. The *toubob* took something from his black bag and stirred it into the water. The black woman kneeled and tilted the cup for Kunta to drink. It had a strange taste, and soon Kunta drifted into deep sleep.

When he awoke he knew that he was very ill. His whole right side felt numb, his lips were parched from fever, and his sweat had a sick smell. Involuntarily, he made an effort to flex his toes; it brought a blinding pain. The door opened, and the black woman came in again. Squatting down, she pressed a damp, cooling cloth against his forehead.

On her next visit she tried to get him to eat. He was even thinner now than he was the week before when Bell, serving the noon meal, was hurriedly called to help lift from a wagon the bloody heap. The sheriff had ordered the slave catchers to deliver it to Dr. William Waller, the brother of Kunta's owner. The doctor, who was Bell's massa, had been livid when he learned of the maiming.

Bell covered Kunta's bare chest with an acrid, steaming poultice of boiled elderberry leaves mixed with sulfur. Then she packed wet cloths over the poultice and covered Kunta with quilts.

When Kunta next awakened, he realized that his fever had broken. He wondered where the woman had learned what she had done. It was like the medicines of his mother, Binta, the herbs of Allah's earth passed down from the ancestors.

His pain became less of an agony now, except for the tall *toubob's* daily treatment of his foot. One day Kunta was untied from the stakes, and he managed to prop himself on his elbows. He spent hours staring at the bandages over his foot stump. For most of his 18 rains (the Gambian way of saying 18 years, based upon one rainy season per year) he had run and climbed anywhere he wanted to go. It seemed monstrous that a *toubob* would chop his foot off.

He took out his rage and his humiliation on the black woman when she came in to feed him, snarling in Mandinka and banging down the tin cup after he drank. Afterward he lay, even more furious, reflecting that the woman's eyes had seemed to warm upon his show of anger.

After three weeks the *toubob* took off the bandages. Kunta almost screamed as he saw the swollen half of his foot covered with a thick, brownish scab. The *toubob* sprinkled something over it, bandaged it loosely and left. Three days later he returned with two stout sticks with forked tops—Kunta had seen injured people walk with these in Juffure.

When the *toubob* had gone, Kunta painfully pulled himself upright and tried the sticks. He managed a few awkward, forward swings of his body. When Bell brought his breakfast the next morning, his glance caught the quick pleasure on her face at the marks the sticks had made on the dirt floor. Kunta glowered at her. He refused to touch the food until she left. But then he ate it hungrily, wanting its strength. Within a few days, he was hobbling freely about the hut.

The Fiddler

In the evening on this farm the black ones gathered at the last hut in the row. It was occupied by a *sasso borro*—a man of about 50 rains who had brown skin, indicating that his father had been white. Listening intently from within his own doorway, Kunta could hear the brown one talking almost continuously. Sometimes the others burst into laughter. At intervals, they barraged him with questions. Who was he, Kunta wondered.

One day as Kunta passed on his crutches, the brown one beckoned him to take a stool by his hut. Kunta sat down opposite the man.

"I been hearin' 'bout you so mad," the brown one said. "You lucky dey ain't kilt you! Law say anybody catch you escapin' can kill you; law say cut your ear off if white folks say you lied. Law 'gainst teachin' any nigger to read or write; law 'gainst nigger beatin' any drums—any of dat African stuff. ..."

Somehow it did not matter that Kunta could not understand. An exhilaration gripped him that someone actually was talking to him directly. And the man simply loved to talk. If he had lived in Africa, Kunta thought, he would be a wandering *griot*, one who told the history of ancient kings and family clans.

Late that night, sleepless, his mind tumbling with inner conflicts, Kunta recalled something his father had once said when he had refused to let go of a mango so that his brother Lamin could have a bite. "When you clench your fist," said Omoro, "no man can put anything in your hand." Yet he also knew that his father would not want him to become like the other black people.

"Looka here!" the brown one said abruptly one afternoon. "You—you Toby!" Kunta's face flushed with anger. "Kunta Kinte!" he blurted aloud, astonished at himself. It was the first utterance to anyone in the more than a year since he had been in the *toubob* land.

The brown one frowned his disapproval. "You is Toby! You got to forgit dat African stuff! Make white folks mad and scare niggers." He looked around the room and picked up an oddly shaped wooden thing with a slender black neck. "Fiddle!" he exclaimed.

In their privacy, Kunta decided to repeat the sound. "Fiddle..." he said tentatively.

The brown one began pointing at other objects—"Bucket...chair...cornshucks"—and Kunta repeated the sounds. After they had gone through more than a score of words, the brown one grunted: "You ain't as dumb as you looks."

The lessons continued. In time Kunta was able not only to understand, but to make himself understood to the brown one, who wished to be called "fiddler."

One day, special shoes were brought to Kunta by a black man called Gideon, who made horse collars and shod the black people. One shoe's front half was stuffed with cotton. Kunta put them on. He felt stinging sensations in his right half-foot as he gingerly walked around his hut, but finally he put his full weight on it and did not

> "You lucky dey ain't kilt you!" the brown man said. "Law say anybody catch you escapin' can kill you."

feel undue pain. He had thought he would always have to walk with crutches.

That same week the fiddler heard from Luther, the black driver, that the *toubob* doctor now owned Kunta. He carefully explained the news to Kunta. "Luther say the massa got a deed to you from his brother who had you at first. Niggers here claim he a good massa," the fiddler continued, "an' I seen worse. But ain't none of 'em no good."

At about this time, Kunta began keeping a calendar by dropping pebbles into a gourd. He guessed he had spent 12 moons on the first *toubob* farm, so he dropped 12 pebbles into the gourd. Then he dropped in six more, making a total of 18 moons that he had been in the land of the *toubob*. Adding the 18 moons to his 17 rains when he was taken from Juffure, Kunta figured that he was now in his 19th rain.

"War Am Ober!"

Soon afterward, Kunta was told by an old black man who worked a small vegetable garden, "Massa put you to workin' with me." He showed Kunta how to hoe the weeds and pick off tomato worms and potato bugs. When the feeble old gardener became ill, Kunta tilled the garden alone.

The season of snow came, and the other blacks were caught up in an increasing excitement about some day called "Christmas." It had something to do with singing, dancing and eating. Kunta overheard talk that Christmas also involved the Allah of the *toubob* and the black ones. It made him ill at ease, and during the days of festivities he did not leave his hut even to visit the fiddler.

Spring came for Kunta, and then summer, in a sweating blur of days as he struggled to plow, plant and cultivate the garden, and supply vegetables to Bell, who was cook for the big house. At night he was too tired to do more than throw himself down on his cornshuck mattress, his clothes wet with sweat, and sleep. Sometimes he still thought of escape, but his impulse to flee was always tempered by the terrible memories of what had happened to him.

When the harvest was in and the fall chores were begun, there was talk of Christmas again. This Christmas, Kunta felt, Allah would have no objection to his merely observing the activities. But the Muslim Kunta was deeply offended when he watched the preparation of liquor from fermented apples. He thought it sickening when the young black ones amused themselves by holding dried hog bladders on sticks close to the fire until they burst. And he was particularly repulsed when Bell supervised the cooking of a large, black iron potful of hogs' jowls and black-eyed peas for the "New Years" of "Sebenteen Sebenty."

"Hog jowl an' peas is good luck!" the fiddler shouted at him, his mouth full. Kunta was disgusted. Sitting on his stool in his hut, he worried that he might find himself easing into an acceptance of the ways of the other blacks. Yet he wanted to know them better—the fiddler and the old gardener and the cook Bell.

One day, on an impulse, Kunta told Bell that she looked like a Mandinka. He meant it in a complimentary way, and he was astonished by her irate outburst: "What fool stuff you talkin' 'bout? Don' know how come white folks keep on emptyin' out boatloads of you black African niggers!"

Bell remained tight-lipped for days afterward. But one morning in March 1770, she came rushing out to the garden filled with excitement. "Sheriff jes' rid off! He tol' massa been some big fightin' up nawth somewhere called Boston! Massa sho' upset." Later Luther, the buggy driver, brought more information. "Dem Boston peoples got so mad at dat king 'crost the big water dey marched on his soldiers. Dem soldiers start shootin', an' first one kilt was a nigger name of Crispus Attucks! Dey callin' it de 'Boston Massacre.'"

From then on Luther brought regular news from slaves, stable hands and other drivers he talked to about the trouble with England. And scarcely a day passed when the field hands did not hear from an adjoining plantation, or a slave passing on a mule, a rising, lingering, singsong, "Yooo-hooo-ah-hoo! Don'tcha hear me callin' youuuu?" Then the nearest field hand would go running to pick up the latest report and would rush back to tell the others.

News of what was happening "up nawth" continued to come in fragments across the changing seasons. As Kunta dropped pebble after pebble into his gourd calendar, he tried to understand it all. It became increasingly clear to him that the *toubob* folks were moving toward a crisis with the *toubob* king. Kunta was especially interested in the thing called "freedom." As best he could find out from the fiddler, it meant having no massa at all, doing as one wanted and going wherever one pleased. But why would the white folks have to talk about freedom, he wondered.

The biggest excitement came with the news late in 1775 that Lord Dunmore, the Royal Governor of Virginia, had proclaimed freedom for slaves who would serve on his fleet of ships and help the *toubob* king. Not long afterward, Massa Waller called Bell to the living room. Twice he read slowly an item in the Virginia *Gazette*. He then ordered Bell to "read" it to the slaves, telling them what it meant. It said that the Virginia House of Burgesses had decreed "…death without benefit of clergy for all Negro or other slaves conspiring to rebel."

"What do it mean?" a field hand asked.

"It mean," the fiddler said dryly, "uprise, an' white folks won't call no preacher when they kills you."

The next summer there was more excitement when Luther returned from the county seat with the news that "all the white folks is jes' carryin' on, hollerin' an' laughin'. Somethin' 'bout some Declaration of Independence."

The old gardener shook his head. "Ain't nothin' neither way for niggers to holler 'bout. England or here, dey's white folks."

In 1778 Bell brought the news that slaves were being promised their freedom if they would join the army as fifers or pioneers. Someone asked what "pioneers" meant. The fiddler replied, "It mean git stuck up front an' git kilt!" And when Bell reported later that two states—South Carolina and Georgia—would not let slaves enlist, the fiddler had a quick retort: "Dat's the only thing good I ever heard 'bout neither one of dem!"

In May 1781 came the astounding story that redcoats on horses had ruined Massa Thomas Jefferson's plantation. Then Luther reported that Massa George Washington's army was coming to save Virginia—"an' niggers aplenty is in it!" That October, the army attacked England's General Cornwallis at Yorktown, and soon came the news that set Slave Row shouting: Cornwallis had surrendered.

"War am ober! The freedom am won!" Bell told everybody. "Massa say gon' be peace now."

"Ain't gon' be no peace!" the fiddler said in his sour way. "Jes' watch what I tell you—it's gon' be worse'n it was—for niggers."

Slave Talk

Shortly after the war ended, Luther helped a slave girl run away. He was found out and sold at auction. Kunta took Luther's place as buggy driver, and the new job vastly broadened his world. Taking Dr. Waller on his rounds, he visited plantations all over the countryside, he saw poor whites, he came into the nearby towns.

In the back yard of one big house he saw a very black woman, who appeared to be of the Wolof tribe. Both of her large breasts were hanging out, a *toubob* infant sucking at one, a black infant sucking at the other. When Kunta later described the sight, the old gardener said, "Ain't hardly a massa in Virginia ain't sucked a black mammy, or least was raised by one."

Speaking to Bell and the fiddler and the old gardener about such things, Kunta was astonished to learn that many white young'uns and black young'uns grew up together and became very attached to each other. The old gardener said that on his second plantation a *toubob* and black boy grew up together until finally the *toubob* young massa took the black one off with him to a William and Mary College.

"He say heap of times dey take dey niggers wid 'em to classes, den dey argue later on whose nigger learnt de most. Dat nigger we knowed couldn't jes' read an' write, he could figger, too, an' 'cite dem poems an' stuff dey has at colleges."

"Lucky if he ain't dead," the fiddler said. "'Cause white folks is quick to 'spicion a nigger like dat be de first to hatch a uprisin' or revolt. Don't pay to know too much."

Sometimes Massa Waller invited a friend to ride with him, and then Kunta's rigid back belied that he heard every word. They talked as if he were not there. Whites seldom shared a buggy ride without expressing regional fears of slave conspiracies and revolts. "We should never have let them bear arms against white men during the war. Now we witness the result!"

Massa Waller went on to say that he had read that more than 200 slave outbreaks and revolts had occurred since the first slave ships came. "But beyond that," he added, "I've seen white deaths that, well, I'll not go into details—I'll just say I've thought them suspicious."

Kunta, in fact, knew as much, or more, of these matters. Black men often met secretly. Right in this county he had heard of black ones who had vowed to kill their massa or missis. He had knowledge of hidden muskets and had overheard whisperings of intended revolts.

Kunta's most consistent source of information, especially from faraway places, was when the massa happened to be in the Spotsylvania County Seat as a mail coach came whirling in. Minutes after the mail sacks and bundles of the Virginia *Gazette* had been dropped off, scores of massas, shopkeepers and other *toubob* men were gathered in clusters, talking and exclaiming, and usually Kunta was within hearing.

His ears filled with the *toubob* folks' fury and dismay at the increasing number of "Quakers" who, according to the *Gazette*, had been encouraging black ones to escape, and more recently had begun aiding, hiding and conducting such runaways to freedom in the north.

Returning home, Kunta told what he had seen and heard, with all of Slave Row gathered at the fiddler's cabin listening to him intently. Bell added that she had just overheard Massa Waller and some dinner guests bitterly discussing the news that slavery had recently been abolished in a northern state called "Massachusetts," and reports that other states near there would do the same. "What ' 'bolished' mean?" a field hand asked.

The old gardener replied, "It mean all us niggers gon' be free, one dese days!"

Mortar and Pestle

In the spring of 1788, Kunta was 38 rains of age. In Africa, he thought, he would have been married and have had three or four sons by this time. But the bride's proper age should be 14 to 16 rains, as in Juffure. He had not seen one black female of this age in the *toubob* land whom he had not considered preposterously giggly and silly.

In fact, the only woman he knew well at all was Bell, who was probably beyond 40 rains. She was also disrespectful of men, and she talked too much. But he remembered how, when he had lain near death, Bell had nursed and fed him, cleaned him when he soiled himself and broken his fever. And she did cook endless good things, grinding her corn by hand, although her stone mortar and pestle obviously did not grind as well as those carved from hard wood by the people of Juffure.

For days Kunta kept to himself, turning everything over in his mind. One evening when the horses were fed, he picked up an old, discarded hickory block, took it to his hut and began carving. He saw in his mind the mortar and pestle which Omoro had made, and which his mother had worn slick with grinding.

Whenever he had free time, he sat in his cabin, chopping carefully around the hickory block with a hatchet, making the rough shape of a mortar. Then he began to carve with a knife. Once finished with the block, he found a seasoned hickory limb, perfectly straight and of the thickness of his arm, from which he soon made a pestle, which fit snugly against the mortar's bottom. He smoothed the upper part of the handle, scraping it first with a file, next with a knife and finally with a piece of glass.

After the task was done, he took the mortar and pestle to Bell's kitchen door and set them down on the steps outside. Catching the thumping sound, Bell turned and saw Kunta limping away. She examined the painstaking carving and was deeply moved. It was the first time in her life that a man had made something for her with his own hands. Indeed, she was not even sure it was meant for her.

> Bell was moved. It was the first time in her life a man had made something just for her.

When Kunta returned in the afternoon to find out if the massa had need of him, Bell blurted out, "What dat?" and gestured toward his gift.

In deep embarrassment, Kunta said, almost angrily, "For you to grind cawn wid."

For the next two weeks, beyond exchanging greetings, neither of them said anything. Then one day Bell gave Kunta a round cake of cornbread whose meal he guessed she had made with the mortar. Grunting, he took the bread back to his hut.

After that they saw each other oftener, and though Bell usually did all the talking, Kunta was drawn closer to her. The next summer he accompanied her and the other blacks to the annual Sunday camp meeting. Although he found the "O Lawd" religion repugnant, he recognized in the others' fervor many of the emotions of festivals back in Juffure. On the way home, with Kunta driving, the black ones began to sing: "Sometime I feels like a motherless chile...a long ways from home...a long ways from home —"

Kunta thought about the times when he had been driving the massa somewhere along a lonely road, and suddenly a sound would rise loudly; it would be some black one somewhere alone in the fields or the woods, who had simply opened his mouth and poured from his soul a single, echoing holler that rang and echoed in the still air. The singing of the black ones, he thought, like his own silence, was a reflection of a terrible yearning.

One morning in August 1789, Bell invited Kunta to eat dinner with her in her cabin. He said nothing. But after work he scrubbed himself hard, using a rough cloth and a bar of brown lye soap. As he carefully put on his clothes he found himself singing softly a song from his village, "Mandumbe, your long neck is very beautiful. …" Bell did not have a long neck, but it didn't seem to matter.

Bell's cabin was the nearest one on Slave Row to the big house. The room that he entered when Bell opened the door had a feeling of coziness with its wall of mud-chinked oak logs and a chimney of handmade bricks. There were two windows and two rooms, one of them curtained off. On a table in the center of the main room there was a jar filled with flowers from Bell's garden. Over the fire, Bell heated some chicken and dumplings which she knew Kunta loved.

When Bell again asked Kunta to eat dinner, she cooked things which Kunta had told her also grew in the Gambia—black-eyed peas, and a stew made with peanuts, and yams baked with butter. As she ground up meal for hoecakes with the mortar and pestle he had given her, Kunta could envision her beating the breakfast grain in Juffure.

One evening, when he again came to dinner, Kunta presented Bell with a mat he had plaited from bulrushes with a bold Mandinka design in the center. "Ain't nobody gon' put dey feets on dat mat!" Bell exclaimed. She took it into her bedroom and soon came back. "Dese was to be fo' yo' Christmas, but I make you somethin' else. …"

Kunta took the gift. One of the finely knitted woolen socks had a half-foot, with the front part a soft woolen cushion. Neither he nor Bell seemed to know what to say. A strange feeling swept over Kunta; her hand sought out his. And for the first time in his 39 rains, a woman filled his arms.

Firstborn and Fā

With Massa Waller's permission, Kunta and Bell "jumped de broom" into slave matrimony on Christmas Eve, 1789. In the simple ceremony in Bell's cabin, with all of the people of Slave Row gathered, they locked arms and solemnly jumped together over a broomstick lying in the middle of the floor. That was all there was to it.

Afterward there was feasting and cheer. Kunta noticed uneasily that Bell was enjoying the wine and brandy which the massa had sent as his gift. Once he overheard her confiding to a woman friend, "Sister Mandy, been had my eye on 'im ten years!" He was mortified.

But Kunta got over that. And in the spring of 1790, when Bell announced that she was pregnant, he was overjoyed. In his mind he could see a small face—a manchild face—peering from a bundle on her back.

The baby came in September. Massa Waller was in the cabin with Bell for more than two hours. Kunta squatted just outside, hearing Bell's anguished moans rise into screams that ripped the quiet of Slave Row before there came an infant's sharp cries. Then Massa Waller emerged. "She had a hard time," he said. "But she'll be fine. You can go in now and see your baby girl."

Kunta's heart sank. A girl. But he limped through the doorway. Bell lay quietly, her drawn face managing a weak smile. Kunta kissed her, and for a long while he stared into the black infant's face. She definitely looked Mandinka. He thought to himself that he could not disappear for seven days, as a new father would in Juffure, to think of a meaningful name for the child; he must decide on one right away.

That night, as he walked the paths where he had first courted Bell, he remembered Bell telling of her greatest grief. Before she was 20 she had been married. But her husband had been killed in an escape attempt, leaving her with two babies. Suspicious of her, her massa had sold Bell away—without the children. "Two li'l gals I ain't never seed since," Bell had said. "Ain't got no dream of where dey is, even if dey's livin' or dead!"

Thinking of this, Kunta chose a name. In Mandinka it meant, "You stay here." He did not tell Bell the name, for by the tradition of his tribe, the baby must be the first ever to hear its name spoken.

The next night, over Bell's protests, Kunta carried his firstborn, snugly wrapped in a blanket, out into the crisp fall air. A short distance from Slave Row, he raised the baby up and whispered three times into her right ear: *Ee to mu Kizzy leh.* ("Your name is Kizzy.") Lifting a corner of the blanket, he bared the small black face to the moon and stars and spoke aloud the words that once, in a village in Gambia, had been spoken to him: "Behold—the only thing greater than yourself!"

ALEX HALEY / ROOTS

The slaves of James Hopkinson at work on his plantation in South Carolina, mid-19th century.

Bell was indignant when she heard the name. "Kizzy? Ain't nobody never heared of dat name! Ain't gon' do nothin' but stir up trouble." But Kunta explained its meaning, and she relented. The next day it was entered in Massa Waller's big black Bible: "Kizzy Waller, born September 12, 1790."

Kizzy was a bright and lively child; and as the years passed, Kunta began teaching her words in Mandinka. "*Fā!*" Kunta would say, pointing to himself, and was thrilled when the child finally repeated the word. As Kizzy grew, he taught her more involved words—his name, Kunta Kinte, and Kamby Bolongo (which was Mandinka for the Gambia River), and Juffure. And he told her about his father, Omoro, and his brothers, and of the Kinte clan as far back as the days of old Mali. Bell sometimes objected; such things would make trouble with the massa, but Kunta insisted.

Her father's gourd of pebbles had a fascination for Kizzy. Bell told her, "Don't never mess wid dem rocks," but Kunta was pleased at the child's interest. Now, each morning after a new moon, he would let her drop the pebble into the gourd.

He told Kizzy of how he had been captured and how he had been brought to this white folks' land. He would picture for her the village of Juffure. He told her story after story, drawing on long-forgotten incidents. She learned fast; she remembered well. Kunta was deeply pleased. "You will have children," he said. "They must know from you where they come from."

This Cruel Land

The world was changing. When Kizzy was only three the cotton gin was invented, and by the time she was ten it was altering age-old patterns throughout the land.

By 1802, the gin had made large cotton plantations in the deep south more and more profitable. Slave traders roamed the roads inquiring of every owner if he had any slaves for sale, and coffles of slaves streamed south toward the black lands of Mississippi and Alabama. Bell reported to Slave Row that the massa said he would never sell any slave—unless that slave broke one of his rules. Kunta remembered Luther, the previous buggy driver. Now that he had Bell and Kizzy to live for, he did everything he could to stay out of trouble.

And yet in one year—1806, when Kizzy was 16—more than 20,000 blacks had been brought into just two states, Georgia and South Carolina. Slaves were selling for unheard-of prices. Even a baby a few weeks old was worth $200.

And one morning in that year, the county sheriff visited Massa Waller. Bell, who was sent from the kitchen while the sheriff spoke to the massa, knew instinctively that something was wrong, and that it somehow involved her. Just before lunchtime, Massa Waller called her in.

His voice was strained and angry as he told Bell the sheriff's news. A young field hand had been captured after running away. Under beating, he had confessed that he had been helped by Kizzy. "You know my rules," he told Bell. "She will have to be sold." Bell fled screaming from the house to her cabin.

When Kunta returned from an errand in the buggy, Massa Waller led him into a small room in the big house. He told him what he had told Bell.

Kunta went to his cabin numbly. He could not really comprehend what the massa had said. His Kizzy—sold away? It was inconceivable. At the sight of Kunta, Bell began screaming, "Ain't gon' take my baby! Ain't gon' sell my baby! Sell he, not my baby!" The truth sank in, and all the bitterness that had ever been in Kunta boiled in him anew, all that he had ever felt of *toubob*, all that he had never ceased to feel in this cruel land.

The sheriff returned in the middle of the afternoon with a slave trader. The trader went inside the house and emerged holding a chain attached to cuffs around the wrists of a weeping Kizzy.

Bell charged from her cabin. "You done dis?" she shouted at Kizzy. Kizzy's face was an agony. It was plain that she had helped the black escape.

"Oh, Lawd Gawd, have mercy, massa!" Bell screamed. "She ain't meant to! She ain't! Please, massa, please! Please!"

Massa Waller spoke tersely: "Wrong is wrong. You know my rules. I have already sold her." He nodded to the slave trader who started to pull Kizzy toward his cart. Then Kunta sprang to his daughter, seizing her about the waist, hugging her as if he would crush her. "Save me, Fā!" she cried.

The sheriff's pistol butt came crashing down against Kunta's head, and he fell to his knees, dazed. Vaguely he saw the slave trader pushing Kizzy, her body thrashing, flailing, into the cart. The cart gathered speed; Bell went lumbering after it, and Kizzy was screaming.

Kunta rushed to where Kizzy had last stood. Bending, he scooped into his hands the dust of her footprints. The spirits said that if he kept that dust, her feet would return to that spot.

He ran with the dust toward the cabin in Slave Row. He must put it in some safe place. His eyes fell upon the gourd full of pebbles. He flung away the dust and, snatching up the gourd, banged it down against the packed-dirt floor. The gourd burst into pieces, and the pebbles which had been his record of the rains of his life went flying in all directions.

"He Were a African"

Kizzy was bought from the slave trader by a man named Tom Lea, who took her to a small plantation in North Carolina. Her new massa forced himself on her, and she bore a child named George. It bothered Kizzy that he was brown, but she learned not to think about it.

By the time he was four, George knew that his grandfather was African. Since few slave children on the Lea plantation even knew who their fathers were, George pestered his mother for more information about the man who had said his name was "Kunta Kin-tay," who called a fiddle or guitar "*ko*," and a river "Kamby Bolongo."

"Where he from?" George would ask.

"He were a African, I tol' you!"

"What kin' of African, Mammy? Where 'bouts in Africa he from?"

Kizzy, remembering how her father had said she must tell her children where they came from, told George how Kunta Kinte had been not far from a village called Juffure, looking for wood to make a drum, when four men had captured him, put him on a ship, and taken him to a place called "Naplis."

In 1827, when George was 21, he "jumped de broom" with a girl named Matilda. Between 1828 and 1840 they had seven children. Each time one was born, George would assemble all the family in his cabin. With the new infant on his knee, the older children gathered about the hearth, he would implant in their minds the story of their great-granddaddy, "the African who said his name was 'Kin-tay,' who called a guitar '*ko*,' and a river 'Kamby Bolongo,' and said that he was out looking for wood for a drum when…"

The children of George and Matilda grew up, each one entering field work as he got old enough, all except the fourth child, Tom, who became a blacksmith. In 1856, Massa Tom Lea fell on hard times and had to sell his slaves. They all went to a tobacco plantation in Alamance County owned by Massa Murray.

There, in 1858, Tom, the blacksmith, married a half-black, half-Cherokee girl named Irene. As Irene had one child after another, Tom did what his father had done, and his grandmother Kizzy before that, telling his children about the African whose name was "Kin-tay." When the hard and bitter years of the Civil War were over, they became free. But they had no land and no place to go, so they stayed at the Murray plantation, the white Murrays and the black Murrays struggling on together.

Then, in 1872, George led a 29-wagon train of black families out of Alamance County, North Carolina, and through the Cumberland Gap to Henning, Tennessee. The last wagon was driven by his blacksmith son, Tom Murray, with his wife, Irene, and their seven children, the youngest a two-year-old girl named Cynthia.

That little girl was my grandma. At her knee I first heard the story of "the African," Kunta Kinte, which led to my search for roots.

Today the Haley family continues to reflect, in microcosm, the changing attitudes and opportunities of black America. Author Alex Haley's father, Simon, worked as a part-time Pullman porter while attending the Agricultural and Technical State University at Greensboro, N.C. In the summer of 1916, making the run from Buffalo to Pittsburgh, Simon Haley was befriended by R.S.M. Boyce, a retired executive of the Curtis Publishing Co. Boyce subsequently provided the funds that enabled Haley to graduate and go on to the New York State College of Agriculture and Life Sciences at Cornell University for a master's degree. Then, Simon Haley taught at small Negro colleges in the South.

Alex Haley's mother, Bertha, was a grammar-school teacher. He has two brothers, George W. Haley, an assistant director of the United States Information Agency; and Julius C. Haley, a Navy architect. Alex Haley himself, since retirement from the U.S. Coast Guard, has pursued an increasingly successful career as a writer of books, magazine articles and screenplays. To further the study of black heritage and genealogy, he and his brothers have established the Kinte Foundation, in Washington, D.C.

What *Roots* Means to Me

I am sometimes asked to explain the success of *Roots*, to pinpoint what it is that this book has touched, and the answer is really very simple. In all of us there is a hunger, marrow-deep, to know our heritage—to know who we are and where we have come from. Without this enriching knowledge, there is a hollow yearning. No matter what our attainments in life, there is still a vacuum, an emptiness, and the most disquieting loneliness.

The whole business of family quest, which is the wellspring of *Roots*, is a great common denominator, a leveler in which a king is no more than a peasant. It reaches into something subliminal in people, and I have been most astonished that the response to it transcends all lines—color lines, age lines, ethnic lines.

Broken chains at the feet of Lady Liberty signify freedom to those who sought refuge on our shores— and serve as a reminder that some of us actually came in chains.

Published in Reader's Digest, May 1977

With the exception of American Indians, we are a land of immigrants. All of us ancestrally come from somewhere across the ocean. Our roots with our immigrant forebears touch the deepest chords within us. When you look at slave-ship scenes, as horrible as they were, you also have to remember the long lines of immigrant ships, with their passengers huddled in steerage, desperately trying to learn a few words of a language that was to be their adopted tongue forever.

n the "Tonight Show," I presented Johnny Carson with his lineage (prepared by the Institute of Family Research, Inc., in Salt Lake City), which told him for the first time that his own Kunta Kinte—the ancestor bridging the sea to the New World—was an indentured servant who worked seven years for a ship's captain to earn his freedom in America. After the Carson show, researchers at the Institute of Family Research received more than 18,000 inquiries seeking clues to people's backgrounds. Personally, I have gotten thousands upon thousands of letters in which the writers pour out their hearts to me, with the one recurring poignant line: *Help me find out who I am!*

Yet, in our nation of immigrants, blacks have been the only unwilling immigrants; the lot of chattel slaves was not comparable to the status of indentured servants. Slavery stole from blacks all insight into what they had been. Now, because of *Roots*, many blacks have said that Kunta Kinte, my forebear, has become *their* ancestor.

And why not? Ancestrally, every black person has the same pattern. He or she goes back to an African—who was born and reared in a village like Juffure, was captured and put into some slave ship, processed through some succession of plantations, on up to the Civil War and emancipation. From that day to this, the black human being has struggled for freedom. That is the constant story for every one of us. There are no exceptions!

Kunta Kinte's story relates this progression, told from the point of view of the victim. For black people, Kunta Kinte is the symbolic, mythological ancestor out of Africa, and with him there is a positive, lineal *Roots* identification. I know of at least 12 newborns named for him, and in San Francisco the mother of twins named one baby Kunta and the other Kinte.

In all of us—black, brown, white, yellow—there is a desire to make this symbolic journey back to the touchstone of our family. In New York, a taxi driver got talking to me about his visit to the Italian town where his forefathers had lived. He started weeping, just recalling what it had been like to step on their soil. He became so emotional that he had to pull over and stop the cab.

About 90 percent of my mail is from whites, and I have yet to receive my first hate letter. The pattern is for the writers to tell me that (1) they are white; (2) *Roots* caused them to realize they had never understood the black condition; (3) the book started them thinking about their own family.

It has been a joy to see this positive identification by whites with what *Roots* is saying. In Los Angeles, a friend of mine overheard young white children arguing over who would get to play the part of Chicken George, one of Kinte's descendants, in their game. None of this would have occurred if for white people *Roots* were a negative reminder of what had been. Instead, it is a positive avenue into a new perception of others, an understanding of a proud African, of a proud people, and the sensitive culture in which they lived. "You have given me," one California woman wrote, "a new awareness of your heritage. The people of Africa came alive and with them their beauty, pride, tradition and strength. Kunta Kinte is now part of me. I will carry him, his family and his country with me and, hopefully, this new awareness will make me a better human being."

Numerous letters from whites say something like, "Thank you that I did not feel hostility. I did not feel you were accusing me, indicting me. I felt you were simply trying to tell me what happened."

This book took me 12 years to write. I relate that to something that my grandma used to say: *The Lord may not come when you want Him to, but He will always be on time*. The book has come at a time of a convergence of social assuagements and a healing political climate. People are starting to find one another, and this is where, for me, the meaning of *Roots* lies.

In this country, we have been like people who live in the same house and tend to stay in our own rooms, doing no more than peeking out and then ducking back. If only we could all come out together, say in the living room, and learn more about each other, we couldn't help but benefit. It would show us our future as a collective people—

> In all of us—black, brown, white, yellow—there is a desire to make a symbolic journey back to the touchstone of our family.

retaining, being proud of, our differences, but coming together in collective strength. That, I believe, is the hope for America.

In my long and troubled journeys to complete *Roots*, I owe an undying debt to *The Reader's Digest*. Without its help and encouragement, *Roots* could not have been written with the scope that it has. The magazine's support enabled me to make repeated trips to Europe and Africa. Without it, I could not have afforded the traveling and, consequently, could not have explored my roots.

Some have wondered why I let *Roots* take 12 years of my life. Rather than *taking*, the book has *added* years—and brought me incomparable rewards. In Los Angeles, more than 3,000 people, white and black, lined up for hours, waiting to get inscriptions in their copies of *Roots*. Exactly five persons had only one copy; the average was three, the peak eight. "This is not a book," one black woman told me, "this is my history." A pregnant black woman handed me two copies to sign. "One," she said, "is for me; the other is for him"—and with that she patted her belly.

My reaction to the heroic status ascribed to *Roots* is that I never felt a greater sense of responsibility in my life. I have an opportunity which few human beings have, to help the influence for good that *Roots* inspires. What the book has done for blacks, particularly young blacks, is to give them an image model. One black told me, "I have always thought the bestseller lists were rigged against us. But with you and *Roots* I can no longer think that."

But *Roots* is becoming a springboard to striving for millions of people, regardless of color. When you see that a goal is attainable, hopefully you are prompted to pay the dues, do the work, and thus pursue the long, hard apprenticeship that is the handmaiden of achievement.

To me, the overwhelming affirmation of *Roots* can be explained only by something that is beyond ordinary comprehension, something spiritual. I think that we as people—and I am talking about the world—badly need uplifting. We all have lineage and forefathers. If I have become a symbol of the shared search for ancestral roots, then indeed am I blessed. ✦

What *Roots* Means to ...

Halle Berry
Oscar-winning actress

Roots totally had an impact on my life because black history wasn't something that we learned in school. It was an education that I think I was always longing for.

I remember a sense of pride after seeing the movie. People knew about it, people were talking about it. Black people, white people, children, adults. It created lots of conversation and a lot of disturbing feelings. But at the same time, I felt a sense of relief because our story, our history, was being told and getting a lot of attention.

Todd Bridges
Actor who portrayed Bud in *Roots*

I was nine when I played Bud. I had a chance to really learn about slavery and what happened to the Africans who were brought over here.

I watched the show with my parents. It made a lot of us sad because we had never really understood our history. I still remember filming the scene where they beat my dad on the tree. That was pretty severe. It got to me. Just to imagine that they actually would do something like that to somebody.

One day I'm going to sit down with my children and watch *Roots*.

Smokey Fontaine
CEO and editor in chief of men's magazine *Giant*

No matter where you were, no matter how old you are, you remember when you were watching *Roots*. It was such an important moment for African American families to have that kind of TV show at that length. That was a really important time.

My mother is African American, my father is British. *Roots* really showed me what our history was about and how rich and meaningful that history is, even though it's a painful history. The vitality and the life that came through that program was so strong, it could really move whoever was watching it, whether it was an African American family or a Caucasian family.

Roots was an American story, and it needed to be told.

Sandy Duncan
Actress who portrayed Missy Anne Reynolds in *Roots*

I grew up in a little town in East Texas. It was very much a part of the Bible Belt and very much a racist area. I came from very liberal parents and grandparents. I remember, I must have been about nine or ten, and my mother and I were in JCPenney. And I was standing there, and I saw this black woman explaining to her little four- or five-year-old kid, because he was in tears, why he couldn't drink out of that particular water fountain. I said, "Mom, why does it say 'For Coloreds Only'?" And I remember my mother sat down and said this is the most hideous thing that exists at this point. She went on and on about how to treat each other. And I wrote a paper about that experience in my school, and I was called nigger lover after that.

I felt privileged to be part of *Roots*. In the miniseries, we were all actors who saw very clearly what they were trying to tell in this story. I think everyone was of the same mind, to bring all of that to light in a very real and personal and graphic way to the American public, people that sometimes tend not to want to look at the truth. If we don't see it, it doesn't bother us somehow.

And so *Roots* was an attempt to make people responsible for humankind.

Judge Glenda A. Hatchett
Star of *Judge Hatchett*

Riveted. There's no other word. *Roots* so profoundly affected not only black America, but white America. It was just an amazing education for all of us.

I was very deeply rooted in my history. I grew up in the Deep South. My parents were always very clear about where we came from. But I think *Roots* put a face on it for me in very graphic ways that I think are very profound.

Robert L. Johnson
Entrepreneur and the nation's first African American billionaire

I grew up with an interest in history, so I was fascinated by *Roots*. To me, it was a walk through history, but his book personalized what I knew and made everything seem far more real than when you studied that particular period in United States history. So to me it gave it more emotional personality.

If *Roots* did anything, it made you recognize that if you were ever going to achieve anything as a black man, you couldn't look for the government to be your ultimate salvation. You've got to do it yourself. You've got to take control of your own destiny because that's what black folks have had to do all their lives.

To his credit, Alex Haley told the story of slavery with about as much passion and reality as has ever been done. And he personalized it.

B.B. King
Blues entertainer

Roots made me have courage. It also made me cry. The courage it made me have was knowing that people of the United States and the world are aware of what happened to my ancestors. I figure most people didn't even think about them.

I was encouraged to read the book after I saw the miniseries. At that time, I was struggling very hard trying to make a living. And it gave me courage to keep trying, knowing that Alex Haley wrote a book and did all this research. It made me want to work harder.

I think it's one of the great turns of history in the lives of Americans. I think it made Americans, black and white, look at ourselves differently. It made us think differently. And I believe if a lot of the kids could see it today, they would see themselves differently, think more of themselves than doing bad things to their own people.

Ed Lewis
Chairman and founder of Essence Communications

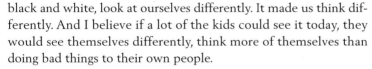

Without question, Alex Haley is one of our icons, one of our heroes. He did so much from the standpoint of opening up an avenue for people to read about our history.

I made an extraordinary effort every night that *Roots* was on to make sure I got home, along with my family, to partake in this extraordinary series. It was just absolutely magnificent for me.

I'd like to think it was an eye-opener for all of us in this country, the role and impact that slavery had on our society. And it's through the extraordinary hard work that the slaves did, how they overcame, how they fought, how they loved, how they took care of their families, the friendships they built. All of that was an eye-opener.

I once asked an extraordinary gentleman, about 85 years old—we were trustees of the Tuskegee Institute—what it is about us as black people that enables us to survive. He looked at me and he said, "Young man, the best explanation I can give you is that we just refuse to die, and our ancestors refused to die."

The courage, the perseverance, the will to survive, to overcome.

I am certainly, like many others, the beneficiary of what our ancestors were able to endure. And what they endured has enabled me to be the kind of individual and leader who wants not only to endure, but to make sure that we have opportunities that all people can partake in.

Vernon Jordan
Senior managing director, Lazard Frères

Roots should be on a family reading list. It told a story that's never been told, really. It's important because white historians have never been accurate or fair. I remember Ulrich B. Phillips saying that slaves were just as happy as they could be. Well, that's nonsense. Alex Haley took us all the way back and allowed us to participate in the journey. It was almost as if we were there with our ancestors. That's certainly what it was for me.

Roots was a bruising reminder of our history and our past, and it was a bruising reminder of man's inhumanity to other men. The message of *Roots* is one of survival and endurance.

Marc Morial
President and CEO of the National Urban League

I was a freshman at the University of Pennsylvania when the miniseries aired. We watched it in the TV room of the dorm. The room was packed, and there was a whole lot of excitement and conversation. *Roots* was a gripping story. You felt everything from anger to pride. And there was a great sense that you were learning and getting exposed to history in a new and different way.

My family was very attuned to our own family history, but *Roots* spurred a great interest in the specifics and details. My father's family came to the United States from Haiti. And my uncle actually had a passage document from 1804.

Kareem Abdul-Jabbar
NBA Hall-of-Famer and author

My great-grandmother emigrated from West Africa to the West Indies in the 1880s. And my great-grandfather was also from the

West Indies. So I know something about the African connection in my family. But to most black Americans, that's a luxury. It's something that's impossible to ascertain.

Alex Haley embodied what most black Americans go through because their whole access to their heritage has been destroyed by slavery. That's a traumatic thing. Haley was able to overcome that, through the research he did. And through sheer force of will.

Dr. Vance Moss
Cardiothoracic surgeon

My twin brother, Vince, and I experienced quite a bit of racism on our path to success. As young guys, we had each other to try to battle this racism, but we still didn't understand why things were happening to us based on our color. And then when we saw the miniseries and then started reading the book, we realized that this has been traditional. This is the way it's been since Africans came to this country.

Roots helped us at least relate to the fact that we're not the only ones experiencing this. The most positive thing we got out of it was how they overcame those obstacles. And that's how we've projected ourselves.

Dr. Vince Moss
Renal transplant surgeon

My brother and I grew up in a middle-class area. We were usually the only African American boys in school or in a Boy Scout troop. My parents were divorced. Everyone else's families were together. *Roots* showed us how these families were separated and sold and how they were able to persevere. It

gave us the impression that it happens, but you shouldn't use it as an excuse.

My mother constantly reminded us of our slavery background. The book gave us an illustration of what it meant to be a slave.

My father made us watch the miniseries. In fact, he bought us the book that week. It's one of the monumental pieces of literature that ranks, in my eyes, with Shakespeare. It is probably the most important book that I've ever read.

Leslie Uggams
Actress who portrayed Kizzy in *Roots*

Roots made me, and every African American, realize that at last somebody was telling our stories and had something to say. That story changed America. As actors, we would walk down the street and people would come up and apologize for not knowing the history of the African American and the terrible things that had been done. Even now, after 30 years, new generations keep discovering *Roots*.

Dr. David Satcher
Former Surgeon General

I was on the faculty at the Martin Luther King Hospital in Watts, South Central Los Angeles, when *Roots* came out. It had quite an impact on me. I had been involved in the civil rights struggles of the '60s in the South, but I saw a different kind of struggle in South Central Los Angeles—the anger, the poverty, the disenfranchisement.

When the *Roots* series came on, it was just an enriching experience, getting in touch with our history in a very positive way and a very realistic way. It meant a lot to me and to my family at that time.

I didn't have a good knowledge of my past. Neither of my parents finished elementary school, so we didn't have a lot of books and discussions about history in our family. There had been some tough times, things that people didn't necessarily enjoy talking about.

Now since *Roots*, the good news is that on both sides of the family, we've had regular family reunions. Now every time we get together, we talk about our history.

Ben Vereen
Actor who portrayed
Chicken George in *Roots*

I heard stories as a young boy about relatives being hanged and lynched and tarred and feathered and about slavery, and yet it wasn't in the history books.

I didn't know who Chicken George was, but I was so happy to be a part of *Roots* because of the importance of the piece. You've got to understand something. In our country, in America, our history, African American history—at least when I was coming up—was not taught. Alex Haley's story and mine were a mystery.

This is a legacy, and being a part of this changed me. It made my career, of course, but personally it gave me a sense of pride.

Henry Simmons
Actor on *Shark* and
formerly on *NYPD Blue*

Ignorance breeds prejudice. It really does. *Roots* was an education for so many people. And in that way, I know that by educating these people, it erased prejudice in some way. It made people more sensitive. I really do believe that.

Dr. Michael L. Lomax
President and CEO,
United Negro College Fund

I had heard Alex Haley speak about the work he was doing during the course of the research and writing of *Roots*. But I don't think anything prepared me for the powerful and dramatic story that I read. Alex was able to make his own personal story, and that of his family, one that embraced all of us. I felt like it wasn't Alex's story anymore. It was the story I had never known about my own past. It really struck me that these were individual lives being lived in horrific circumstances, yet people still managed to find meaning and dignity in everything. I walked away from the book and the miniseries with tremendous pride. I felt for the first time that slavery had not diminished us.

Slavery is something no one talked about in my family. There was a lot of miscegenation, and there was a feeling of embarrassment. But after *Roots*, I needed to know my family stories; I had to find out. For the past 30 years, I've been involved in genealogy. I now know who my great-great-great-grandparents were and where they lived and how they lived. I feel connected to them, and I know how they shaped my experiences. I don't think I would have gone on that journey had I not read *Roots*.

As African Americans, we owe an extraordinary debt to *Roots*. The book still resonates. The miniseries still has a kind of spine-tingling impact. But now we are able to write our own roots, and we owe that wonderful gift to Alex Haley.

General Colin Powell
Former Secretary of State

The power of *Roots* is that it gave historic dimension to the African experience in America. We just didn't suddenly arrive at Jamestown. We came from somewhere. We had names and homes and families and a background and a culture and a lineage that went back thousands of years. Alex Haley succeeded in making it real for all of us, not only for black Americans but especially for white Americans.

One of the things I've often said about the civil rights movement of the '60s is that it's not only what it did for black people, it's what it did for white people. They got rid of this terrible burden they were carrying called *segregation*. It was a burden, and finally through the power of law, they were relieved of that burden and they could start to reach out to blacks.

Then along comes *Roots* about 12 years later, and it brings a dignity to African Americans that was not obvious. *Roots* gave persuasive evidence and reasons why we should never have been treated as property, because we had the same kind of dignified backgrounds and lineage as any white Anglo-Saxon European coming from England or any-where else. So *Roots* brought us to a peer level of equality with our white brothers and sisters.

I say to young people who wring their hands about the past, you've got to move on. Yes, we were once looked down upon as blacks, but don't let that be a burden for us now.

The reason I became a general and a Secretary of State is because of the sacrifices that were made by African Americans before me. They didn't make these sacrifices so that when I reached this level I could con-tinue to resent history, but that I learn from history, build on our legacy and convey that to the next generation. Be proud of your roots and move onward. ✦

COURTESY COLIN POWELL

WHAT ROOTS MEANS TO ...

As a contributor to *Reader's Digest* for nearly four decades, Alex Haley touched the lives of millions of Americans through his writings. The 30th anniversary of *Roots* inspired us to publish—for the first time—this important collection of his timeless works, which broaden our nation's understanding and appreciation of the African American experience.

All of us who worked on this book and accompanying DVD felt a renewed sense of pride in *Reader's Digest* for having had the courage to feature the original *Roots* excerpts and such groundbreaking articles as "The Man Who Wouldn't Quit" and "Mr. Muhammad Speaks." Our commitment to breakthrough journalism continues to this day, along with our unshakable belief that regardless of race, ethnicity or class, we are all more alike than we are different.

While much about the magazine has changed since Haley was a contributor, *Reader's Digest* continues to offer inspiring stories that celebrate humanity through dramatic accounts of personal triumph. I invite you to pick up a copy of the magazine or visit rd.com.

Jacqueline Leo
Editor-in-Chief